LIFE EXPLORES

The Roaring '20s

THE DECADE THAT CHANGED AMERICA

Piloting the *Spirit of St. Louis,* Charles Lindbergh arrived in the U.K. after completing the first solo flight between New York and Paris, in May 1927.

Contents

TALE OF THE TAPE An official in Washington, D.C., checked that bathers' suits met the locally mandated length of no more than six inches above the knee, 1922.

A Measure of Time

They called them the Roaring '20s, and roar they did, with an intensity that still commands our attention a century later.

Yearning to escape the shadows and gloom of World War I, young people broke with their parents' musty Victorian morals and grabbed at unheard-of freedoms. Women, emboldened by their newly won right to vote, not only expressed their opinions but also danced, wore daring new fashions and, yes, even smoked. The brashest of the bunch, known as flappers, became the symbols of the glamorous era.

Business boomed, and a consumer culture flourished, spurring Americans to buy flashy cars and new time-saving household appliances. A lucky few became fabulously wealthy, spending on breathtaking mansions, sprawling yachts and vacations to exotic destinations around the globe.

Meanwhile, everyone danced. And when they did, it was to jazz, ragtime and the blues, the sounds that formed the decade's soundtrack. White and black audiences alike thronged nightclub dance floors to shake and shimmy to the energy of the music. Radio and new national media gave rise to a cult of celebrity, and athletes such as Babe Ruth and movie stars like Greta Garbo were transformed into household names.

The strictures of Prohibition just added to the fun. Millions of Americans blatantly broke the law by patronizing speakeasies or making their own liquor. Even the rise of organized crime could not put a damper on the exuberant mood. Americans just wanted to transgress. The Great Depression would bring the party to a crashing halt, of course, but the world had changed in radical ways, and there was no going back. ■

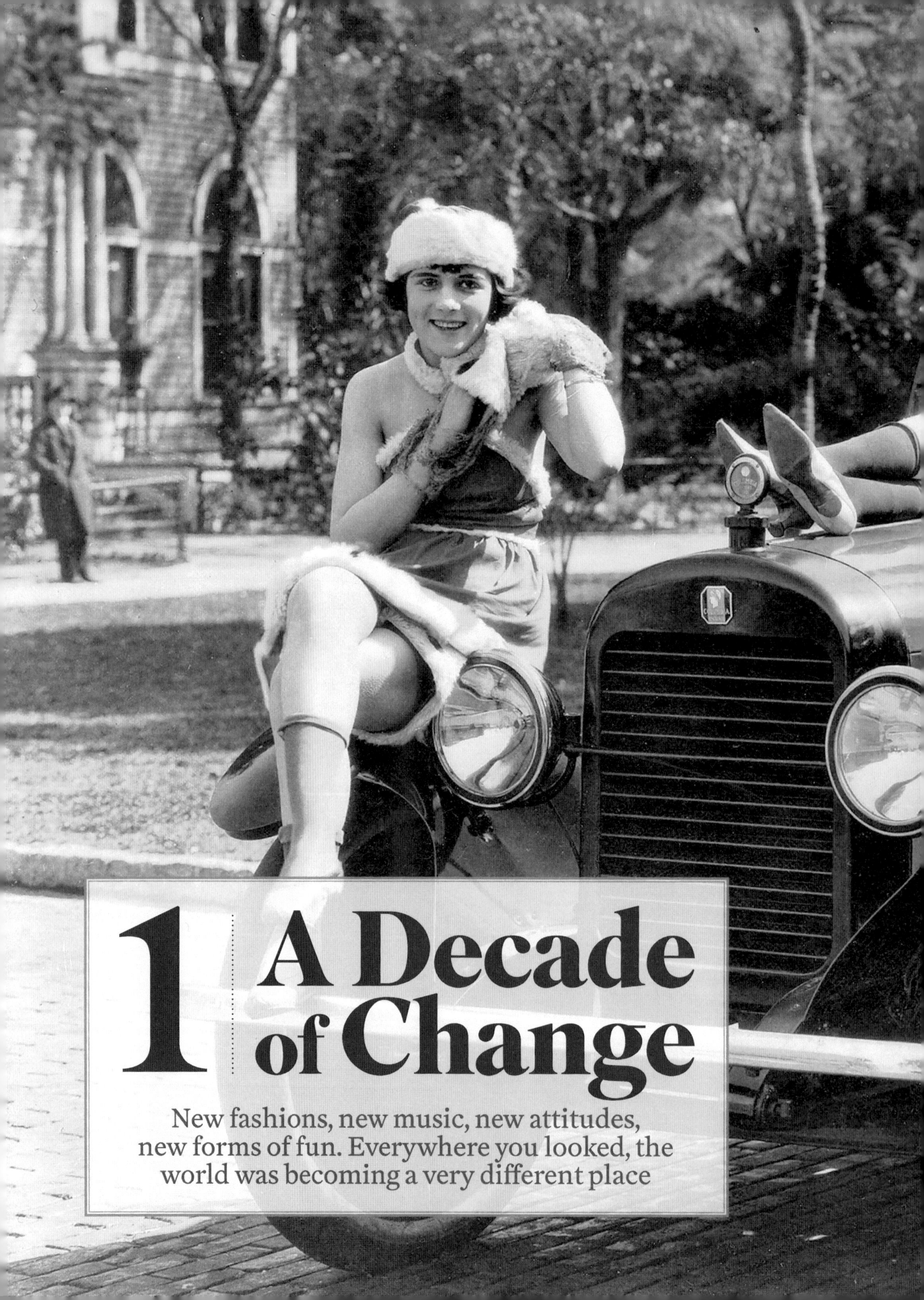

1 A Decade of Change

New fashions, new music, new attitudes, new forms of fun. Everywhere you looked, the world was becoming a very different place

Bathing beauties in Florida circa 1920.

WINDY CITY HIGH JINKS
Two flappers (right) danced the Charleston on the ledge of Chicago's Sherman Hotel in 1922. The same year, the Chicago police (below) arrested a bathing-suit-clad young woman for indecent exposure.

Cultural Revolution

The parties were wild, the jazz was hot, the fads were completely off the wall—and there was a new topic: sex

Maybe it was inevitable after the dark days of World War I: As the 1920s got under way, Americans plunged headlong into an era of unadulterated hedonism. The watchword of the decade was fun, pure and simple, in pretty much every form imaginable.

In cities all across the land, parties—fueled by illegal but widely available quantities of alcohol—seemed almost continuous. If a private event could not be found, frivolity was always on tap in the speakeasies and jazz clubs, where patrons danced the night away, intoxicated by the new rhythms emerging from African-American musicians like the great Louis Armstrong.

The new music and the glittering venues brought with them shifting attitudes too, particularly among the young, who rejected their parents' notions—outmoded, in their view—of what constituted proper behavior for chivalrous gentlemen and modest ladies.

> ***"Of all the crazy competitions ever invented, the dancing marathon wins by a considerable margin of lunacy."***
>
> —THE *NEW YORK WORLD*, 1923

Women embraced the new freedoms, cutting their hair, applying makeup and tossing out dowdy fashions of the past for shorter skirts and slinkier, more form-fitting attire.

Then there was the sex. Once the seismic insights of Sigmund Freud crossed the Atlantic, Americans jumped at the chance to talk about this formerly taboo subject. The revealing clothes, the sensuous dances and the more open attitude toward physical contact between the sexes represented a revolution. "Necking" in the back of a car on a deserted road might not seem particularly daring to modern readers, but in the 1920s such activity was seen as positively scandalous.

The endless search for the new spawned a host of fads. Two young publishers, Richard L. Simon and M. Lincoln Schuster, brought out a collection of puzzles as their first book, and the nation's obsession with crosswords was born. Contract bridge, yo-yos and roller-skating became popular. Millions of Americans—women in particular—began playing mah-jongg, an ancient Chinese game that blended dice and dominoes. A former sailor called Shipwreck Kelly became a celebrity for flagpole sitting, spending untold hours on a small platform atop an 18-foot pole in venues throughout the eastern United States, frequently advertising for a hotel or theater. Dance marathons, in which contestants did the Charleston and Lindy hop until they dropped from exhaustion, became common. "Of all the crazy competitions ever invented, the dancing marathon wins by a considerable margin of lunacy," reported the *New York World* in 1923.

The end of the decade would bring many of these lighthearted pursuits to a crashing conclusion, but, in the words of a popular song from the era, "in the meantime, in between time, ain't we got fun!" ■

LAISSEZ-FAIRE POLITICS

Pro-business Republican presidents ruled the White House for a decade

1920 IN THE PRESIDENTIAL election, the progressive internationalist politics of incumbent Woodrow Wilson were soundly defeated in a race between two dark-horse candidates from Ohio. Democrat James Cox was an activist in Wilson's mold, and Republican Warren Harding promised a "return to normalcy." Harding won in a landslide. Wilson died a broken man in 1924.

1923 WARREN HARDING, whose administration was marked by scandal, died of a heart attack and was succeeded by Calvin Coolidge. Harding's secretary of the interior, Albert Fall, eventually went to jail for accepting bribes in exchange for leases to drill on federal land in California and Wyoming. The episode was dubbed the Teapot Dome Scandal, in reference to the location of the oil reserves in Wyoming.

1924 CALVIN COOLIDGE won election in his own right. He impressed the American people with his moral rectitude and promised to keep the prosperous times rolling by leaving business alone. Famously taciturn, Coolidge explained his reticence this way: "I've noticed that nothing I've never said ever did me any harm."

1929 HERBERT HOOVER became the third in the series of pro-business Republican presidents. Responding to the 1929 stock market crash, Hoover proposed economic half-measures that failed to resolve the crisis, helping to propel Franklin Roosevelt to the White House in 1932.

VIEW FROM THE TOP
Alvin "Shipwreck" Kelly, the sailor-turned-flagpole sitter, settled in for a session in Union City, N.J., in 1929.

DRIVE, SHE SAID The British-made Rolls-Royce (right) was a status symbol for the rich. Publisher Condé Nast captured the decadence of the leisure class in a fashion shoot (below).

The Rich Are Different

From French châteaux to fur chapeaux, newly minted millionaires indulged their every whim. Oh, to be a Morgan or a Rockefeller!

Income equality and the danger it poses to the social fabric feels like a contemporary problem. But the gap between the rich and everyone else was never greater than in 1928, when the most prosperous 1 percent of American households controlled 51.4 percent of the nation's wealth. (Today's one-percenters control about 40 percent of the country's wealth.) The booming economy, marked by increases in productivity, sales and wages, fueled enormous corporate profits. In 1923, U.S. Steel was operating so efficiently that it was able to reduce its workday from 12 to 8 hours, employ 17,000 additional workers and raise wages—all while building up the immense fortune of founder J.P. Morgan. Similar scenarios unfolded in many of America's other burgeoning industries, from automobiles to home goods.

"We are a happy people—the statistics prove it. We have more cars, more bathtubs, oil furnaces, silk stockings, bank accounts than any other people on earth."
—HERBERT HOOVER, MARCH 1929

The gross national product increased from $74 billion in 1921 to $104.4 billion in 1929. Who cared if the rich were getting richer? Lots of Americans were.

But of course, the rich were getting a lot richer than everyone else, mostly because of the explosive growth of the stock market, where large family fortunes grew truly enormous. Titans like Standard Oil founder John D. Rockefeller increased their portfolios simply by holding on to large quantities of stock in their own companies. Other investors thrived on sheer speculation.

Many of these fortunes came tumbling down at the end of the decade, when in the course of a few weeks, the stock market crashed and burned.

It started in late September, when prices began to decline, but it was on October 18 that they took a real dive. By the 24th, on what became known as Black Tuesday, panic had set in on Wall Street, and prices went into free fall. Investors—mostly wealthy types but also ordinary Americans—desperately began attempting to sell their portfolios. Five days later, on October 29, the market collapsed completely. More than 16 million shares changed hands, as brokers made "margin calls" demanding that investors pay the difference between the minimal amounts they put down to buy shares (often as little as 10 percent) and the actual purchase price of the investment. The vast majority of people simply did not have the cash available to cover the difference. Almost $15 billion went up in smoke on that single day, forever known as Black Thursday.

Contrary to popular belief, the stock market crash did not cause the Great Depression, but it pointed the way for the chaos that followed, as factories, farms, and banks closed en masse. The Roaring '20s roared no more. ■

TRINKETS FOR THE SUPER-RICH

Those who made the most money proved adept at spending it too. The impetus was not need but simply desire

STOCK TICKER
No self-respecting tycoon could survive without a stock-market ticker to keep track of his many holdings. This early self-winding model, invented in 1923, was later replaced by Western Union's high-speed ticker, which could record 500 characters per minute.

MASSIVE MANSION
Lavish homes have always been on the shopping lists of the wildly wealthy. This château-style mansion belonged to the Vanderbilt family and was located on Fifth Avenue and 58th Street in New York City. It took up an entire block.

SAILING YACHT
Nothing announced an arriviste's wealth like entering a 150-foot sailing boat in a British regatta. This race, near Great Britain's Isle of Wight, took place in 1927.

ROLLS-ROYCE PHANTOM I
The Rolls-Royce—with a $10,000 price tag—was the car of choice for the millionaire set (Jay Gatsby, in *The Great Gatsby*, drove a yellow Rolls "of monstrous length"). There were also more exotic autos, such as the Italian-built Isotta Fraschini 8A Boattail Tourer, which retailed for $14,500, or $194,000 in today's dollars.

A Gathering Storm

Resentment among those left out of the decade's prosperity created toxic conditions

HIDDEN BENEATH the glamour and the glitter lay a harsh reality: the prosperity of the go-go '20s was hardly universal, even leading to extremism. Farmers, lumbermen, New England textile workers, coal miners in Pennsylvania and many other ordinary Americans suffered. Mired in poverty, African-American sharecroppers in the South streamed northward in search of better lives.

The face of America was changing. Millions of immigrants arrived on U.S. shores from Italy, Ireland and Eastern Europe. By 1920, after decades of largely open borders, almost 14 million residents—or 13 percent of the U.S. population—were foreign-born, a fivefold increase from 1850.

This shift spawned a decidedly ugly brand of politics. The Ku Klux Klan emerged as a force, with membership reaching a high of 4 million in 1924. Calling for "100-percent Americanism," the group expressed hatred for African Americans, foreigners and anyone who was not a native-born white Protestant. Other nativist organizations flourished as well, and in 1921 and 1924, Congress passed the nation's earliest immigration-quota laws restricting both the number of immigrants allowed into the country and the nations from which immigrants would be accepted.

VICTORY AT LAST In 1920, after Tennessee became the 36th state to ratify the 19th Amendment, suffragette Alice Paul unfurled a banner with 36 stars to celebrate. Finally, enough states had ratified the amendment to make it the law of the land.

Liberated

With the new right to vote, women began to express themselves at the polls. They also took up vices that had long been the provinces of men: smoking, drinking and all-around bawdy behavior

As the decade began, women took to the streets to celebrate the passage of the 19th Amendment, granting them the vote. Newly empowered and energized, women were soon making their presence felt in the popular culture, frequently in unconventional guises. Flappers, jazz babies, brazen stars of the silver screen—these were women with opinions, who expressed their desires and their sexuality.

Many discarded the corsets and girdles of yore and even went braless beneath the new fashions, which emphasized a girlish, athletic figure and suggested a woman ever on the go. Bright lipstick, colorful eye shadow and smoky mascara were introduced in the 1910s, but the new cosmetics became more widely available in the '20s and offered women

NATIONAL

"She was beautiful—but especially she was without mercy."

—F. SCOTT FITZGERALD, *THE BEAUTIFUL AND THE DAMNED*, 1922

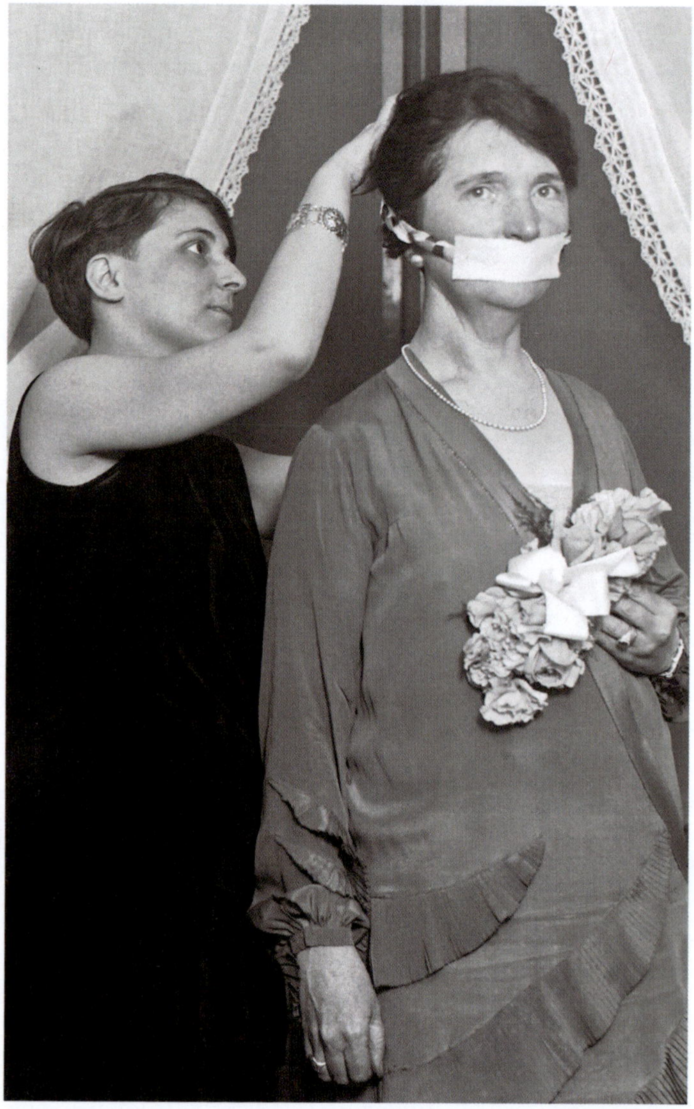

POTENT PROTEST **Women's health advocate Margaret Sanger published numerous books on the benefits of modern birth control, like the one advertised above. After Boston mayor James Curley banned Sanger from speaking about the topic within the city limits, she protested by appearing at a Boston theater in 1929 with a gag over her mouth (right).**

another means of bold expression. Every pharmacy and department store now sported a makeup counter. Movie star and "It Girl" Clara Bow made the flaming-red Cupid's-bow upper lip and smoldering dark eyes the signature look of the era, and millions of women followed suit.

As women grew more assertive and more independent from men, they also embraced a nontraditional view of sexuality, one divorced from procreation. Condoms, which had become popular with U.S. armed forces during World War I, were more widely available, and other forms of birth control, like the diaphragm, caught on. Women's health activist Margaret Sanger founded the American Birth Control League, the precursor to Planned Parenthood. A sexual revolution was afoot. ■

Sell Them Their Dreams

To keep consumers spending, the advertising industry stretched the truth and tapped into hidden emotions

THE MIRACLE of mass production, which made it possible to manufacture affordable automobiles, unleashed a dazzling array of consumer goods. There were vacuum cleaners that replaced brooms; refrigerators that allowed consumers to keep food fresh for long periods of time; washing machines that rendered wringers obsolete. The "labor-saving" devices had the unintended effect of raising standards of cleanliness and creating more housework, but the businesses fostered new jobs and higher wages. Those in turn helped create the very consumers needed to support their operations.

Of course, for consumer society to flourish, the public had to know where to direct these new dollars, and so the modern advertising business was born. It started in print, with colorful compositions that sold the notion that a particular product (kitchen cabinets, a stylish bathroom or a sleek automobile) would endow the purchaser with a previously unimaginable level of status. Some celebrated miraculous time-saving appliances. Others offered relief from socially damaging conditions like halitosis. Many ads trafficked in quasi-factual pseudoscientific details: a mouthwash boasted the approval of exactly 45,512 doctors. Testimonials featuring celebrities who vouched for a product (for fees of up to $5,000) caught on as well.

But the decade's dominant trend was tapping into the secret emotions that motivated people to buy. One poetic advertisement for a product that remains an American staple to this day offered this bit of inspiration: "Each day tends down hill from that top-of-the-morning feeling with which you begin. Don't whip yourself as the day begins to wear. Pause and refresh yourself with an ice-cold Coca-Cola and be off to a fresh start....It is ready, cold and tingling, at fountains and refreshment stands around the corner from anywhere." Who could resist?

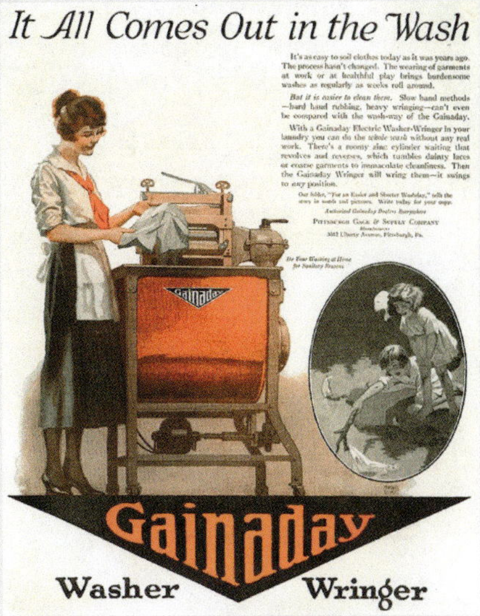

Boats and planes greeting the S.S. *Berengaria* in New York Harbor in 1926. The ship carried Gertrude Ederle, who had just become the first woman to swim across the English Channel.

2 Getting Around

America was on the move, and so was the transportation industry. Detroit cranked out cars. Luxury liners crisscrossed the Atlantic. And then came the planes

CAR CULTURE Assembly workers at the Ford Motor Co. plant (right) in Dearborn, Mich., put the last touches on a new car. To tank up, owners headed to filling stations, like H.H. Hart Garage in California (below).

The Automobile Age

Mass production made cars more affordable, and soon Americans of even modest means were traveling the roads

It's nearly impossible to overstate the impact that the automobile had on American society. First, there was the economic effect: Henry Ford's production lines, as well as those of other carmakers, employed some half a million Americans in the 1920s, providing them with steady, predictable and rising incomes. The fast-growing industry also spawned ancillary businesses. Steel production skyrocketed. Manufacturers needed tires, glass, leather and brake systems. The finished product required fuel, filling stations and roads for its journeys across the land. Car ownership nearly tripled, rising from 8 million registered vehicles in 1920 to 23 million by the end of the decade.

Equally important was the new mobility offered by the game-changing machines. Americans could live farther from their places of employment, which greatly increased job opportunities and enabled businesses to recruit across wider geographic areas. A more mobile citizenry felt free to shift locations entirely, ushering in an era of large-scale migrations. The passage of the Federal Highway Act of 1921 meant Americans had 96,626 miles of interconnected roads to travel on. Suddenly they could take vacations in previously unreachable locales, a development that transformed the tourism industry.

More broadly speaking, the '20s marked the beginning of the American love affair with the automobile. It's a romance that persists to this day, fed by a driving culture born at a time when motels, gas stations, roadside cafés and tourist attractions began to populate the U.S. landscape. ■

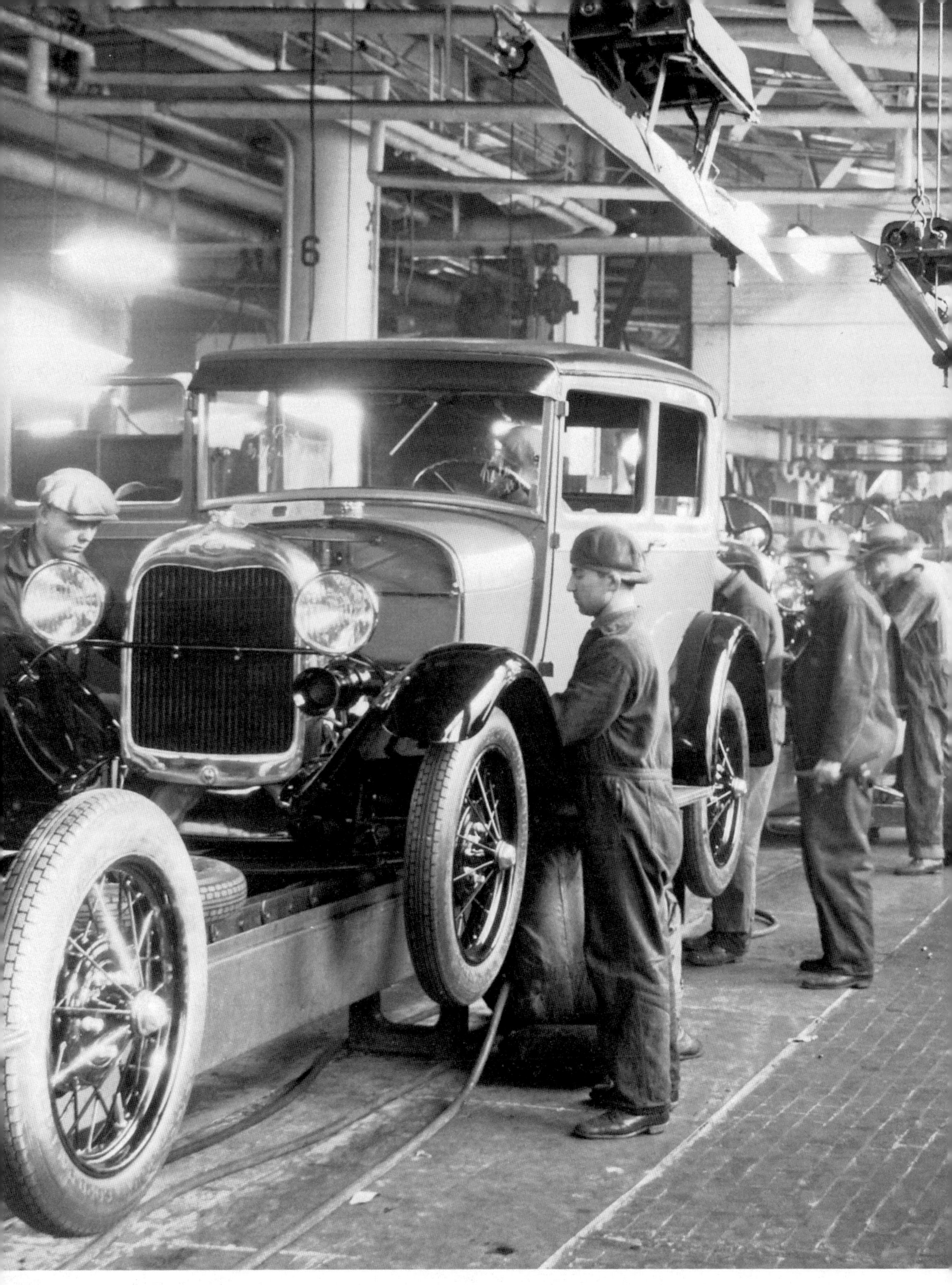

PLUCKY PIONEER Lindbergh in 1927. Following his historic transatlantic flight, he worked to promote the budding aviation industry.

Lucky Lindy

In the first solo transatlantic flight, Charles Lindbergh battled fatigue, heavy fog and an ice storm, but he touched down in France a hero

In 1927, flying toward Europe in the *Spirit of St. Louis,* Charles Lindbergh wondered if anyone was following him and the progress of the first solo transatlantic flight. Little did the aviator know that upon reaching France he would be greeted by 150,000 delirious Parisians, who caused one of the largest traffic jams in their country's history. Will Rogers captured the seriousness of Lindbergh's accomplishment when he announced to readers in his syndicated column: "No jokes today… a slim, tall, bashful, smiling American boy is somewhere over the middle of the Atlantic Ocean, where no lone human has ever ventured before…."

From the very beginning, the flight was fraught with danger. Departing from a muddy runway at New York's Roosevelt Field at 7:52 on the morning of May 20, Lindbergh's plane was barely able to maintain takeoff speed. The plane, heavy with the weight of gasoline Lindbergh needed for the lengthy trip, lurched under the burden. It finally lifted off, just missing a stand of trees near the runway by a matter of yards.

Over the Atlantic, Lindbergh struggled to stay awake as his plane repeatedly dipped to within 10 feet of turbulent waters. Blinded by heavy fog at one point, Lindbergh found himself flying directly into an ice storm. He adjusted his route before the plane's engines started to freeze over. Then, at 10 p.m. on the second day of his flight, Lindbergh saw the lights of Paris in the distance. He touched down at Le Bourget airport at 10:21 on May 21, forever earning the sobriquet Lucky Lindy.

Over the next few years, Lindbergh worked to promote airmail service and the nascent commercial airline business. But his fortunes changed in 1932, when his 20-month-old son, Charles Jr., was kidnapped and then murdered. In what became known as the "Trial of the Century," a German immigrant carpenter named Bruno Hauptman was convicted and executed for the crime. Soon afterward, partly in order to escape the glare of publicity, Lindbergh left the country. Accompanied by his wife, Anne Morrow, and their second son, Jon, he moved to England. Positive prewar comments about Nazi Germany tarnished Lindbergh's image in subsequent years, but he supported America's entrance into the war after the attack on Pearl Harbor and flew 52 combat missions in the Pacific. In the 1950s, he served as a consultant to the U.S. Air Force and to Pan American World Airways. Both he and Morrow were much admired for their later environmental efforts. ■

of

POST TO PASSENGER Two women (right) became the first official Boston-to-New York passengers in 1927 when they paid $25 each to ride on a mail-delivery plane. Workers loaded mailbags onto an early delivery flight (below), circa 1920.

The Friendlier Skies

The commercial airline industry began with a ragged band of barnstormers and the decision to deliver the nation's mail by air

The commercial passenger aviation industry didn't really take off until the 1930s, but its foundations were established in the late teens and the 1920s. It started with the airmail business. In 1918, nine years before Lindbergh's historic flight, the United States Post Office Department sanctioned the delivery of mail via air.

The first official route, which had its own stamps, was the Washington to Philadelphia to New York corridor. Due to ill-equipped planes and unreliable weather reports, the death toll in the early years was appalling: 31 of the first 40 pilots to fly the mail from New York to Chicago were killed in crashes. By 1921, the safety record had improved, and the first batch of transcontinental mail was delivered via a series of coordinated flights. Added together, the flights took 33 hours and 20 minutes, an accomplishment that persuaded Congress to continue subsidizing the mail effort. As routes lengthened and safety and reliability improved, the public grew more confident in air travel. What's more, a once-skeptical business com-

"The life of an aviator seemed to me ideal. It involved skill. It brought adventure. It made use of the latest developments of science."

—CHARLES LINDBERGH, 1927

PLANES TAKE OFF The all-metal Ford Tri-Motors (below) were reliable and reasonably priced—Ford eventually produced 199 of them. Henry Ford lost interest in the aviation business when Douglas developed superior planes in the 1930s.

munity began to consider that a commercial passenger industry might be feasible.

By the mid-1920s, the postal service had essentially developed its own airline, which largely traveled along a well-established—and now mostly safe—transcontinental route between New York and San Francisco via Chicago. When the government decided to expand this service by offering delivery contracts to 12 independent operators, the commercial aviation industry was born. Over time and through a variety of mergers, these early operators would morph into Pan Am, Delta Air Lines, Braniff Airways, American Airlines, United Airlines, Trans World Airlines, Northwest Airlines and Eastern Airlines.

Early on, these companies mostly stuck to carrying the mail, in large part because there were no aircraft that could safely transport more than a handful of passengers. That changed in 1925 when Ford Motor Co. bought out the Stout Aircraft Co. and began mass-producing the all-metal Ford Tri-Motor, an affordable, reliable airliner that could carry up to 12 passengers. Suddenly the airlines and their financial backers could see a way to carry enough paying customers to make the business model reasonable. Western Airlines, which later merged with Delta, started the first regularly scheduled airline passenger service in 1926, between Salt Lake City and Los Angeles.

Many obstacles remained. Old airports, many of

Behemoths of the Air

The gigantic dirigibles once seemed indestructible

SOME OBSERVERS were convinced that the huge dirigibles, which were fueled by hydrogen and able to transport more passengers than single-wing aircraft, would become the carriers of the future.

There was reason to be hopeful. In 1919 the British Royal Air Force's airship *R34* made the first round-trip Atlantic crossing, from Scotland to New York and then back to England. By 1929, the *LZ-127 Graf Zeppelin* (pictured here), a German dirigible, had completed the first round-the-world passenger trip. The ship eventually flew more than a million miles and carried more than 34,000 passengers.

But as single-wing aircraft became faster, able to carry more passengers and safer, the dirigible began to lose its luster. Sealing its fate was the 1937 *Hindenburg* disaster. Attempting to dock in New Jersey, the vessel inexplicably burst into flames, killing 36 people. The public's faith in dirigibles was shattered.

them built quickly to accommodate airmail service, had to be adapted to handle the new planes and the longer runways and landing strips they needed. More-sophisticated facilities were required to handle the growing number of commercial passengers. And somehow the fear of night travel had to be conquered. A first step was a cross-country effort that involved plane travel by day and train by night over an exhausting 48-hour period. Developments in the 1930s, including the construction of sleek new airports, more-efficient, safer planes—most notably the Boeing 247 and the Douglas DC-3—and the introduction of approach lighting on runways, solved most of these problems. Eventually airlines also brought down costs, which made it possible for many middle-class Americans to take their first flight. ■

SIDESHOW TO BUSINESS
Passengers step through a rear entry door on a Tri-Motor (top) in 1928, the same year Pan Am began advertising its flights from Miami and Key West to the Bahamas and Cuba (above).

AERIAL ACROBATS

Many Americans experienced flight by watching the exploits of fearless barnstormers

During World War I, Americans thrilled to the exploits of fighter aces like Eddie Rickenbacker, whose midair, man-to-man battles with German pilots put a human face on combat. But after the war, many of these hero aviators struggled for relevance in a peacetime economy. Some turned to barnstorming, staging daring aerial exhibitions on war-surplus trainers. The planes, completed too late to see service, could be bought for as little as $300 each.

One favored maneuver was the barrel roll, a combination of a loop and a roll in which the plane rotated, first on one axle, then on the other. Another was wing-walking: Stuntman Wesley May famously crouched on the top wing of a plane with a gasoline can strapped to his back while another plane flew alongside, wingtip to wingtip. Then May stepped across to the other plane, walked the length of its wing and calmly poured the fuel into its tank.

INTO THIN AIR In 1921, stuntman "Fearless Freddie" clung to a rope ladder as he prepared to leap to a waiting car below.

SEA AND RAIL **Pullman upgraded its sleepers (right) to satisfy wealthy travelers, while ocean liners like the S.S. *Aquitania* (below) became more accessible to middle-class travelers.**

Old Standbys, New Luxuries

When Americans set out to see the world, they wanted to do so in style. Railcar makers and luxury liners met the challenge

Even as sexy new cars and planes began to entice Americans on the move, ships and trains continued to carry the largest number of travelers.

To attract increasingly affluent customers, railcar maker Pullman began upgrading its famous sleepers in the 1920s. Along came the single room, with full toilet facilities, a stationary bed across the car, an electric fan, a folding washstand and a drop table for eating and writing. Passengers of means could purchase an adjoining room, if desired, to create an entire suite. Pullman also improved its dining cars, adding elegant touches, such as silver-plated flatware, bold new china patterns and a menu with more than 100 offerings, including orange juice that was squeezed to order. In 1929 the company introduced air-conditioning, an amenity that was available in half of all Pullman sleepers by 1937.

A similar phenomenon unfolded on the high seas, where ocean liners had traditionally catered either to the well-to-do heading abroad or to foreigners fleeing to America for the chance of improving their lives. Once immigration quotas were introduced in 1921, shipowners had to switch gears. Many retrofitted their craft to attract customers who weren't super-rich but who expected more comfortable accommodations than those once offered in steerage. A trip to Europe or a cruise to an interesting spot such as the Mediterranean or the West Indies became an envied status symbol. ■

Young smokers in Long Island, New York, circa 1925.

3 Bright Young Things

Dancing, dating, smoking, showing off in daring fashions: The flappers and their friends changed all the rules

GIRL DESCENDING
In 1927, Suzette Dewey (right), daughter of banker Charles Dewey, represented the epitome of flapper chic.

Yes Sir, That's My Baby

Young, carefree and always on the lookout for the next party, the flapper was the great symbol of the age

Much of what we associate with the 1920s reflects the passions of a youthful generation in revolt against the stodgy rules of its elders. In 1920, journalist John F. Carter Jr., writing in the *Atlantic Monthly*, described the prevailing attitude this way: "I would like to observe that the older generation has certainly pretty well ruined this world before passing it on to us. They give us this Thing, knocked to pieces, leaky, red-hot, threatening to blow up; and then they are surprised that we don't accept it with the same enthusiasm with which they received it."

This rebellion had its most vivid expression in a cheeky group of women who became known as flappers. They were young. They liked to drink, sometimes to excess. They smoked, openly and without shame. They wore makeup, sometimes including flaming-red lipstick and eyes heavily lined with black mascara. They loved to dance to the wild new rhythms. And they went to so-called petting parties, where they pushed the limits of what had previously been considered ladylike behavior. Testosterone-fueled boys and young men were happy to contribute to this more liberated spirit, of course, as their own adolescent rebellion now found much freer expression.

The petting parties were especially scandalous to the older generation, though in fact their public nature tended to keep them relatively tame. "Certainly there were parties where young people did quite a lot of erotic exploration—kissing and fondling," cultural and social historian Paula Fass told NPR in an interview. "These parties always stopped before intercourse.... They allowed young people to experiment in a self-limiting way by creating peer regulation that both encouraged experimentation and created clear limits." The carefree flappers and sheiks—as the men were sometimes known, in tribute to dashing film star Rudolph Valentino—even had a name for this behavior: "snugglepupping."

"The pace was faster, the shows were broader, the buildings were higher, the morals were looser, the liquor was cheaper..."

—F. SCOTT FITZGERALD, 1932

PAIRED UP Petting parties like this one, circa 1928, scandalized older generations.

The old folks were not amused. Police in Atlantic City, New Jersey, threw ice water on petting parties on the beach; in Pittsburgh, 15 couples were fined for spooning, the *Reading Times* reported in 1921. Such attempts at repression were futile. The kids did what they wanted, then as now, though as the decade wore on, their frivolity morphed into cynicism. "The parties were bigger," wrote F. Scott Fitzgerald, commenting on the social scene in New York City at the time. "The pace was faster, the shows were broader, the buildings were higher, the morals were looser, the liquor was cheaper; but all these benefits did not really minister to much delight. Young people wore out early—they were hard and languid at twenty-one.... The city was bloated, glutted, stupid with cake and circuses, and a new expression 'Oh yeah?' summed up all the enthusiasm evoked by the announcement of the last super-skyscrapers." ■

JAZZ AGE LEXICON

Ever tell a friend she's a pushover? Did she tell you to scram? You've been using '20s slang. Here is some of the best-known lingo of the era:

all wet \ôl wet\ *adj*: wrong; arguing a mistaken notion or belief
bee's knees \bēz nēz\ *noun*: a superb person or thing
bel•ly laugh \belē laf\ *noun*: a loud, uninhibited laugh
big cheese \big chēz\ *noun*: an important person
blind date \blīnd ˈdāt\ *noun*: a date with an unknown person, usually arranged by a mutual friend
bull ses•sion \ˈbu̇l ˈse-shən\ *noun*: an informal group discussion
cat's me•ow \kats mē-au\ *noun*: a highly admired person or thing
crush \krəsh\ *noun*: a strong feeling of romantic love for someone that is usually not expressed and does not last a long time
fall guy \fȯl ˈgī\ *noun*: a scapegoat
hard-boiled \ˈhärd-ˈbȯi(-ə)ld\ *adj*: tough; without sentiment
horse•feath•ers \ˈhȯrs-ˌfe-thərz\ *noun, plural*: nonsense, balderdash
ja•lopy \jə-ˈlä-pē\ *noun*: an old, often dilapidated car
main drag \mān ˈdrag\ *noun*: the most important street in a town or city
push•over \ˈpu̇sh-ˌō-vər\ *noun*: a person or thing easily overcome
ritzy \ˈrit-sē\ *adj*: very fashionable and expensive, often in a showy way, from "Ritz," the Paris hotel
run•around \rə-nə-ˌrau̇nd\ *noun*: a deceptive or delaying action, especially in response to a request
scram \skram\ *verb*: to leave hurriedly (from "scramble")
spif•fli•ca•ted \spif(ə)lə ˌkātəd\ *adj*: drunk

RED HOT Flappers tried the latest culinary craze in Chicago's White City amusement park in 1925.

SENSE AND SEDUCTION **The stylized postcard at right, circa 1920, hints at the illicit passions unleashed by the outrageous practice of "dating."**

The Dating Game

The old rules were swept away as young women and men began exploring romance away from the supervision—and the prying eyes—of their parents

The concept of dating, as we understand it, really began in the 1920s. Before then, the more appropriate term for the interaction between unmarried teenagers and adults was courtship, a carefully controlled dance in which the families of a potential couple assessed the appropriateness—largely in terms of social class—of a potential mate. The meetings were held in fully supervised settings, usually in one of the families' homes, and watched over zealously by the parents. The purpose of this ritual was very clear: to move adolescents in a well-defined, straight line from young adulthood into marriage. There was little romance in this approach—and even less fun.

All that began to change in the years after World War I, when a new generation rejected Victorian values and embraced a more liberated lifestyle. With the growing popularity of the automobile, young people discovered not only mobility but also ample opportunity to escape the prying eyes of parents. They listened to the radio and watched movies that fostered a romantic ideal that would become the norm in American popular culture: love, or at least powerful attraction, should be the guiding principle behind a relationship, not prosaic concerns about money or social class. The dramatic theme of star-crossed lovers who prevailed against the disapproval of convention-bound society became one of Hollywood's most successful tropes, and audiences took the message to heart.

Finally, the enormous movie palaces and clubs of the era provided the cover of darkness, where young people in love, or just lust, could be either alone or almost fully hidden.

In this new social order, it became normal to have a boyfriend or girlfriend, not necessarily as a way station to marriage but simply as a means to explore an attraction of some kind, any kind. A girl might have a host of boyfriends before finding "Mr. Right," some of them selected precisely because her parents did *not* approve, making the act of dating a form of rebellion in itself. Boys were thrilled to be free of the need to get parental permission to ask a girl out, happily playing the field and sometimes dating more than one girl at a time—an act that would have been considered completely unacceptable in earlier decades. Parental influence waned by the day. ■

THE UNDER WORLD Women donned sleeker, body-skimming styles, like the V-neck lamé dress (right) worn by Marion Morehouse, wife of poet E.E. Cummings, circa 1925. To do so, they shed girdles and "foundation garments" (below, in a window display circa 1925).

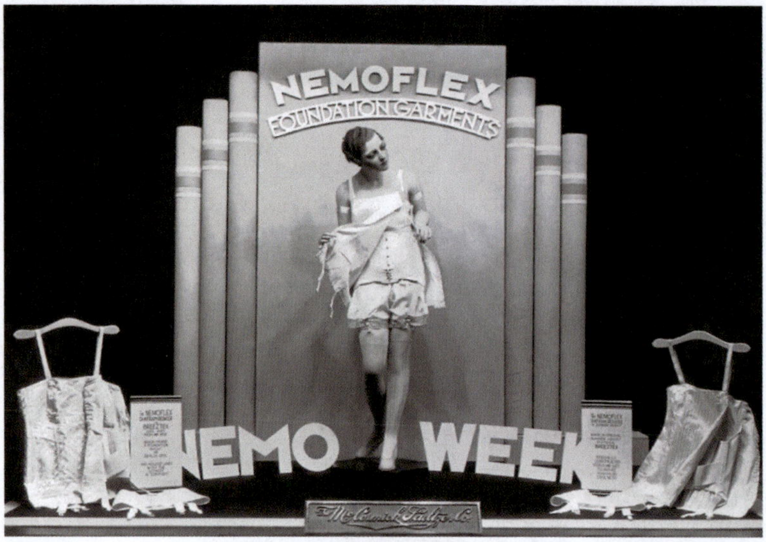

Those Shocking Fashions

Silky, chic and provocative, the 1920s styles broke rules and showed off the assets of a newly confident American woman

The more liberated, assertive, active woman of the era needed new clothes to reflect her changing status, and designers like Coco Chanel and Elsa Schiaparelli stepped in to produce them.

To describe the fashions as revolutionary barely does them justice. Out went heavy wools and practical cottons; in came luxurious silks and satins and less-expensive synthetics like rayon. Designers used the drapey fabrics to create lighter, thinner, less architectural dresses and separates. Waistlines dropped, hemlines rose, and a new, straighter, more athletic profile, sometimes with no waist at all, emerged as the preferred look. Clumsy buttons and lacing were replaced with hooks and eyes and snaps and, easiest of all, zippers. Out too were the bulky and constrictive undergarments of the past, like waist-cinching corsets and girdles; in were light one-piece chemises and camisoles and new, simpler bras. The overall look has often been described as "boyish" due to the straight lines and the short bobbed hair, often topped by the head-hugging cloche. But the styles, colorful and patterned, were far more athletic than masculine. The overall impression was

"A girl should be two things: classy and fabulous."
—COCO CHANEL

OUT AND ABOUT **"Gay Northeasterners Strolling," circa 1920s by James VanDerZee. Three members of an African-American social club, now known as the Northeasterners, promenaded in Harlem.**

just what was intended: women were on the move.

Men's fashions became more athletic too, as sports stars like golfer Bobby Jones and tennis star Bill Tilden became style icons, influencing young men in particular to wear knickers and sweaters, or loose white flannel trousers and V-neck sweater-vests. Formal three-piece suits for business attire gave way to lower-waisted jackets, wider lapels and looser, more comfortable trousers. Softer, more relaxed shirts with attached collars became the norm.

The younger generation was quicker than the older one to adopt the new trends. But by decade's end, women and men of all ages had embraced the stylish designs, which mass production made affordable even for the middle class. Modern fashion, with its accessible, high-end-inspired designs, was born. ■

F. Scott Fitzgerald, Ernest Hemingway and the Lost Generation

Writers portrayed Americans as fast-living, spiritually alienated and disillusioned

FOR WRITERS and intellectuals in America, the frivolity of the 1920s masked a growing sense of unease. F. Scott Fitzgerald was only 24 when his first novel, *This Side of Paradise,* was published in 1920, making him an overnight sensation and establishing him as the preeminent chronicler of the age. Suddenly millions of Americans were reading about the wild young women known as flappers, presented by Fitzgerald as jaded and more than a little cynical. *The Great Gatsby* (1925) depicted a lavish Long Island social scene, which was populated by the rich, the wannabe rich and the phonies like protagonist Jay Gatsby, whose entire personality was an invention, based on nothing but his own imagination. No matter how hard Fitzgerald's characters partied, nothing could conceal their fundamental dissatisfaction with a world gone wrong somehow.

Ernest Hemingway, too, presented a view of what his friend and fellow writer Gertrude Stein called the "Lost Generation." His most memorable works were a pair of semiautobiographical novels: *The Sun Also Rises* (1926), based on a trip Hemingway took to Spain with

GENTLEMEN, START YOUR TYPEWRITERS
Fitzgerald (left, with his wife, Zelda, who became almost as celebrated as he was) and Hemingway (below) both wrote important novels that questioned the boundless optimism of the age.

"I am always in love."
—Ernest Hemingway, *The Sun Also Rises*, 1926

a collection of British and American expatriates, and *A Farewell to Arms* (1929), based on his time as an ambulance driver in Italy during World War I. Like Fitzgerald's characters, Hemingway's were world-weary and disillusioned, but in soldiering on, they presented a portrait of heroism Hemingway admired.

The decade was studded with literary lights. Sinclair Lewis wrote novels like *Main Street* (1920) and *Babbitt* (1922) that skewered the stifling conventions of the American middle class. H.L. Mencken, the nation's leading iconoclast, wrote essays that lambasted all forms of self-righteousness and piety with unmitigated gusto. And onstage, Eugene O'Neill lifted American theater out of vaudeville and saccharine sentimentality with timeless and profound dramas like *Anna Christie* (1921), *Desire Under the Elms* (1924) and *Strange Interlude* (1928). His plays dealt with serious subjects, such as insanity, murder, suicide and death. Many of them were set in the context of the family, an institution O'Neill often viewed as horribly destructive.

"To me, the tragic alone has that significant beauty which is truth," O'Neill wrote. "It is the meaning of life—and the hope."

THEY GOT THE MOVES Siblings James and Louise Sullivan (right) wowed the judges and placed first in the 1926 National Charleston Championships in Chicago's Trianon Ballroom. Club-goers (below) danced the Charleston in 1926 at New York City's Parody Club.

Dancing Fools

Suddenly everyone had rhythm and the footwork to go with it. Americans scuffed up the hardwood as they learned the Charleston, the Lindy hop and the turkey trot

Yes, the flappers most certainly did dance. So did everyone else, as music filled the clubs, dance halls and private parties to overflow. The steps of the day had names like the black bottom, the shimmy and, most famous of all, the Charleston. There were also the Lindy hop, the waltz, the tango, the turkey trot, the buzzard lope and the chicken scratch. Most involved a lot of movement accompanied by actions that would once have been considered inappropriate, like a man putting his hands on a woman's hips, or a woman shaking her upper torso. Many of the moves originated in the African-American community, some even beginning as slave dances, then crossed over to white audiences.

The music, too, by and large boasted African-American roots, though most of the songs were actually ragtime, not "jazz." Some of the popular titles remain well known today: "Yes Sir, That's My Baby," "Baby Face," "Where'd You Get Those Eyes" (known

"Not much money, oh but honey, ain't we got fun?"

—RICHARD A. WHITING, GUS KAHN AND RAY EGAN, 1921

to many as "Jeepers Creepers"), "If You Knew Susie Like I Know Susie," "Ain't We Got Fun" and on and on. The American songbook is full of compositions from the 1920s.

The dances were not difficult to master, but they did call for considerable energy. The turkey trot (known later as the foxtrot) involved hopping from side to side and kicking the feet in a scissors-like motion; the shimmy required dancers to shake their shoulders while alternately leaning forward and back, in time with the music; and the Charleston typically featured lots of sideways motion of the limbs (either rapid-fire kicking or sliding of the feet) while facing forward, along with syncopated bending of the knees and waving of the arms, all in time to an infectious beat.

Fun, fun, fun, it was indeed. ■

À L'AMÉRICAINE Famed club owner Joe Zelli (above, far right) brought the American-style jazz scene to Paris, where his Royal Box, opened in 1920, became the place to be.

CIGARETTE CHIC

Smoking became a popular—and fashionable—practice

It's hard to believe that there was a time when celebrities and other influential cultural figures endorsed cigarettes and smoking. Politicians, athletes and even doctors offered their support for one brand or another. The hard sell began in earnest as women took up smoking to assert their independence, and tobacco companies recognized a new target market. One advertisement urged women to "reach for a Lucky instead of a sweet," suggesting they smoke to keep slim.

Hollywood got into the act too, depicting stars smoking on camera and off, which lent glamour to the practice and helped tobacco companies spread the gospel of cigarettes to the masses. Smoking became highly fashionable, with the cigarette attaining the status of an accessory on par with the cloche or a pair of silk stockings. There is no denying the success of these efforts: the number of women ages 18 through 21 who began smoking tripled between 1911 and 1925, and more than tripled again between 1925 and 1939.

ALL THE RAGE The sharing of a cigarette was a sensual gesture for the elegant, well-heeled set, like the couple below in 1928.

The St. Louis Cotton Club Band, circa 1928.

4 All That Jazz

It wasn't just different beats, notes and rhythms. The new sound captured the mood of the nation

SUBLIME SOUNDS By 1927, the jazz action had shifted to New York City and hot spots like the Cotton Club in Harlem (right). King Oliver's Creole Jazz Band, including Oliver (below, third from left) and Louis Armstrong (front), thrilled Chicago audiences.

Big Sound from the Big Easy

The party started in New Orleans, but soon music lovers in Chicago, Kansas City and New York were swaying and stomping to the syncopated rhythms of jazz

The sizzle of the Jazz Age took the country, or at least the country's youth, by storm. Dressmaking establishments advertised "jazz styles," poets wrote "jazz poetry," flappers gyrated to "jazz dances." Serious composers got into the act too. Darius Milhaud, a leading French modernist, wrote a ballet with jazz rhythms, while his countryman Maurice Ravel published a sonata with jazzy passages; German Paul Hindemith weighed in with jazz piano suites; and America's great songwriter George Gershwin produced "serious" jazz compositions, including the unforgettable "Rhapsody in Blue."

But this symphonic jazz and most of the other music that passed for jazz in the '20s was not the authentic article. The real music was being produced in relative

M&S
DOUGLAS
COTTON
CLUB
ENTRANCE
ON LENOX AVE
OVES
OF
RMEN
PRINGLE LEW CODY
IN TEA FOR THREE
GEORGE OBRIEN & VIRGINIA VALLI
EAST SIDE WEST SIDE
A NEW CHAPTER OF THE 2ND SERIES OF
"COLLEGIANS"

"If you have to ask what jazz is, you'll never know."

—LOUIS ARMSTRONG

FORGOTTEN STAR Band leader and jazz pianist Fletcher Henderson (below, right) may not be as well remembered as peers like Duke Ellington, but in his time he was considered among the most talented of all.

obscurity. It had moved upriver from New Orleans, its birthplace, but it was still mainly heard in black dance halls in Harlem and Chicago and on so-called "race records," sold only in African-American neighborhoods.

For those in the know, the foremost practitioner of the genuine art form was King Oliver's Creole Jazz Band, a Chicago-based ensemble with a who's who of great musicians. In 1923, the band included Johnny Dodds on clarinet and his younger brother, called Baby, on drums. Joe Oliver, the cornet-playing leader, was the famous brass man, but now he had with him a cornet sensation from down home named Louis Armstrong. Oliver and Armstrong (who later switched to the trumpet) seemed to read each other's minds, and when they did duets, the crowd at Chicago's Lincoln Gardens went wild, standing on tables and shouting.

Oliver was a powerful man of formidable girth. When he was about to blow something really hot, he announced to the admirers around the bandstand, "Now you'll get a chance to see Papa Joe's red underwear!" As he honked chorus after chorus, his stiff shirtfront would pop open and reveal his trademark red undershirt.

Unfortunately, Lincoln Gardens, like other locales, had to deal with more than just appreciative audiences. Since many of the clubs were owned or controlled by the Mafia, any conflict between rival factions might lead to visits from disgruntled and heavily armed gangsters, sometimes including members of Al Capone's mob. When fighting or shooting erupted, it was the band's job to play as loudly as it could to cover up the noise of shattering bottles or gunfire. Despite the violence, the clubs were where true jazz found an increasing audience and its own real voice. ■

Satchmo and the Empress of the Blues

Two of the greatest stars to emerge from the Jazz Age were Louis Armstrong and Bessie Smith

LOUIS ARMSTRONG hailed from one of the toughest neighborhoods in New Orleans. His parents were indifferent at best, and after he fired a pistol on New Year's Eve in 1913, Armstrong was committed to a reformatory at age 11. The young musician survived his teenage years by working an assortment of odd jobs by day—hawking coal from a mule-drawn cart, delivering milk, working on a junk wagon—and playing jazz in rough cafés at night. His largest single source of income was tips from prostitutes who paid him to play the blues on his plaintive horn.

Armstrong's star began to rise in 1922 when he joined Joe Oliver in Chicago, where his soaring solos and distinctive trumpet tone influenced the course of jazz forever. Playing at the largely black dance hall Lincoln Gardens, Armstrong quickly became a magnet to white audiences too, and he started to cross over to the mainstream. When Armstrong jumped ship, moving to the Fletcher Henderson Orchestra in New York, fans were not far behind, and soon his recordings were playing on radio stations all over the country. By the time of Armstrong's death in 1971, he was among America's most beloved and popular entertainers.

BESSIE SMITH grew up poor too, in Chattanooga, Tenn. She lost both parents and two brothers by age 9. As a teenager, Smith supported herself on the streets by busking for tips in front of the White Elephant Saloon in the heart of Chattanooga's African-American community. At age 14, she caught the eye of the legendary singer Ma Rainey, who hired her initially as a backup dancer but quickly became an important mentor. Smith released her first record in 1923, and it wasn't long before her powerful yet soulful contralto made her the highest-paid black entertainer of the decade and earned her the title of Empress of the Blues.

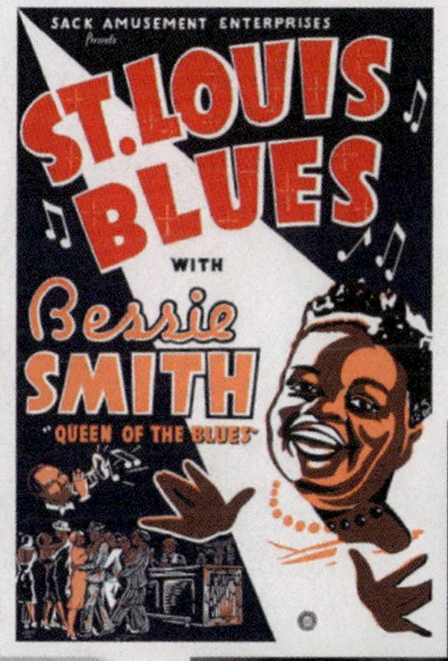

Like Armstrong, Smith found ways to reach mixed audiences. In October 1923, she sang for an all-white crowd in Memphis before heading over to radio station WMC for a performance likely heard over the airwaves by listeners of every color. While her style was distinct from Armstrong's, she influenced his music, as he did hers, and in 1925 Satchmo and the Empress recorded together.

Smith died in a car crash in 1937 near Clarksdale, Miss., regarded by many as the birthplace of the blues. She was only 43 years old.

THAT'S ENTERTAINMENT The nattily dressed waiters of Smalls Paradise in Harlem (below, left) sometimes worked on roller skates. Smalls was one of the only clubs with an African-American owner and one of the few to be integrated (below, right).

Club Land

The joints were jumpin'. With the infectious sounds of big bands, dance orchestras and singers like Ethel Waters, how could they not be?

As jazz caught on, so did the clubs where the music was played. Chicago, Kansas City and New York became hubs for the new sounds, but few areas were more famous for jazz than Harlem. Whites began to flock uptown to the African-American neighborhood to catch elaborate revues that offered, in the vivacious verbiage of *Variety,* "pep, pulchritude, punch and presentation." In 1921, when a group of African Americans penned, produced and performed *Shuffle Along,* a jazz musical on Broadway (revived to acclaim in 2016), it became a smash hit. Within four years, *Shuffle* was followed by eight other black productions, including *Liza, Runnin' Wild* and *Chocolate Dandies.*

Broadway audiences had never known music like this or seen such dancing or heard such singing. They wanted more, and the big Harlem clubs obliged with chorus lines, comedians, singers like Ethel Waters, nimble dancers such as Bill "Bojangles" Robinson, and jazz bands led by Duke Ellington and Fletcher Henderson. Nightclubs like Connie's Inn and the Cotton Club catered to wealthy white customers, while other hot spots welcomed Harlem's own people. Two venues in particular, the Savoy Ballroom and the Lafayette Theater, became the centers of African-American nightlife. By decade's end, there were more than 500 jazz joints in Harlem, and audiences both black and white went home at night humming the irresistible new music. ■

Radio Days

Clubs may have helped popularize jazz, but it was a new device that made the music mainstream

THE RADIO was a game changer for popular entertainment, allowing Americans across the country to discover music, follow sports and keep current with the news. But the early models were prohibitively expensive. A tabletop console could cost $50 to $75 in 1925—that's about $700 to $1,000 in today's dollars—while a cabinet version might run as high as $135 to $175, or half the price of a new Model T Ford. That meant families, and sometimes entire neighborhoods, shared, often gathering in a single home to hear their favorite programs. Most popular in the early years were musical revues and variety programs that mirrored the vaudeville shows of the period. Later in the decade, classic comedies like *Amos 'n' Andy* began to appear.

As more Americans were exposed to radio's wondrous programming, sales skyrocketed. Between 1922 and 1930, the number of families owning radios soared from 60,000 to 13,750,000. With advertisers jumping aboard to sponsor popular shows, radio became a lucrative business. The public was as curious about pitches for products like Wheaties and Pepsodent Tooth Paste as it was about the favorite shows of the time. But there were also vocal opponents who would forever feel that the airwaves belonged to "the people." Dr. Lee De Forest, whose invention of the three-element vacuum tube was critical to the success of big-time radio, complained in 1940 in an open letter to the National Association of Broadcasters that advertising had reduced a promising medium to money-grubbing. "What have you done with my child? You have sent him out on the street in rags of ragtime to collect money from all and sundry. You have made of him a laughingstock of intelligence, surely a stench in the nostrils of the gods of the ionosphere."

TUNING IN Early radios came in a variety of shapes and sizes, including consoles like this one that functioned as stand-alone pieces of furniture.

NEW YORK NOTES A happy flapper (right) put up a poster advertising Paul Whiteman's appearance at the Greenwich Village Halloween Ball; Gershwin (below) began playing the piano professionally at age 15.

Going Mainstream

White performers who were inspired by jazz—or just trying to ride its coattails—began to incorporate the new rhythms and sounds into their own music

As the exciting new sounds started to gain attention nationally, white artists began appropriating the music and adapting it for their own audiences. In some cases, this represented a genuine admiration for jazz; in others, it was simply an attempt to profit off the latest craze.

George Gershwin most certainly fell into the first category. As an 8-year-old, he roller-skated through Harlem to 134th Street and sat on the curb outside Barron D. Wilkins's club and listened to the ragtime rhythms drift out the door. His great tribute to jazz, "Rhapsody in Blue," dubbed "symphonic jazz," was sublime and certainly reflected jazz's technical creativity. The New York City premiere in the winter of 1924 may have been the most celebrated musical event of the decade, with crowds filling the famous Aeolian Hall on 42nd Street to the rafters. Everyone had an opinion afterward, with critics split between those rabidly in favor or against—there seemed to be no middle ground.

Gershwin was first and foremost a songwriter—arguably the most brilliant in American history—who produced iconic compositions like "Lady Be Good," "I've Got a Crush on You" and "Someone to Watch Over Me." The songs became standards for jazz performers, who often used Gershwin's unforgettable melodies as the starting points for their wondrous improvisations.

PAUL WHITEMAN
HIS SUPPER CLUB ORCHESTRA

"It don't mean a thing if it ain't got that swing."

—IRVING MILLS AND DUKE ELLINGTON, 1931

LET'S SHAKE **The jovial Whiteman (above, at right) welcomed guest musician Maurice Hughes to his orchestra in 1920.**

At the less authentic end of the spectrum was chubby bandleader Paul Whiteman, whose widespread popularity seems a bit strange in retrospect. A young violinist from Denver, Whiteman went East in 1920, and by 1922 he was commanding $25,000 for a six-night engagement, an enormous sum at the time and one that was unmatched for decades. Whiteman sometimes had a genuinely talented musician or two, like cornet virtuoso Bix Beiderbecke, in his band, but otherwise it was a mediocre group. Perhaps Whiteman can best be understood as one in a long line of mainstream synthesizers, like Pat Boone and Lawrence Welk, who offered bland renditions of rawer, more authentic American sounds. Whiteman's most important contribution may have taken place behind the scenes, where he championed black musicians and bandleaders. That support prompted Duke Ellington to declare in his autobiography, "Paul Whiteman was known as the King of Jazz, and no one as yet has come near carrying that title with more certainty and dignity." ■

A TROUBLED LEGACY

Al Jolson was among the era's most popular entertainers

No discussion of music in the 1920s could be complete without mentioning Al Jolson, perhaps the most popular performer of the era. Jolson's dynamic, nearly histrionic style thrilled audiences for three decades. His earliest successes were in Broadway musicals, then in clubs and finally in movies, including his appearance in the first "talkie," *The Jazz Singer*, in 1927.

Jolson performed many of his most popular songs, like "Swanee," "My Mammy," "Rock-A-Bye Your Baby with a Dixie Melody" and "Toot, Toot, Tootsie," in burnt-cork makeup, known as blackface. This shameful practice was popular with audiences at the time, and some even considered it a tribute to African-American musicians. Jolson himself justified his routine as a way to challenge the second-class status of African Americans and to underscore the ugliness of racism. His blackface stage persona, Gus, for example, was a clever, wisecracking servant who was always at least one step ahead of his stupid white masters. A Jewish immigrant from Lithuania, Jolson was also noted for fighting discrimination on the Broadway stage and in the movies, and he counted black artists like dancer Bill "Bojangles" Robinson and pianist-songwriter Eubie Blake as friends.

Still, Jolson is often remembered just as the singer who performed in blackface. To the extent that he participated in that tradition, it seems unlikely that his reputation will ever be fully rehabilitated.

PERIOD PIECE Producers of the first talkie, *The Jazz Singer*, promoted the film with images of Jolson performing in blackface.

Babe Ruth with President Warren Harding in 1923.

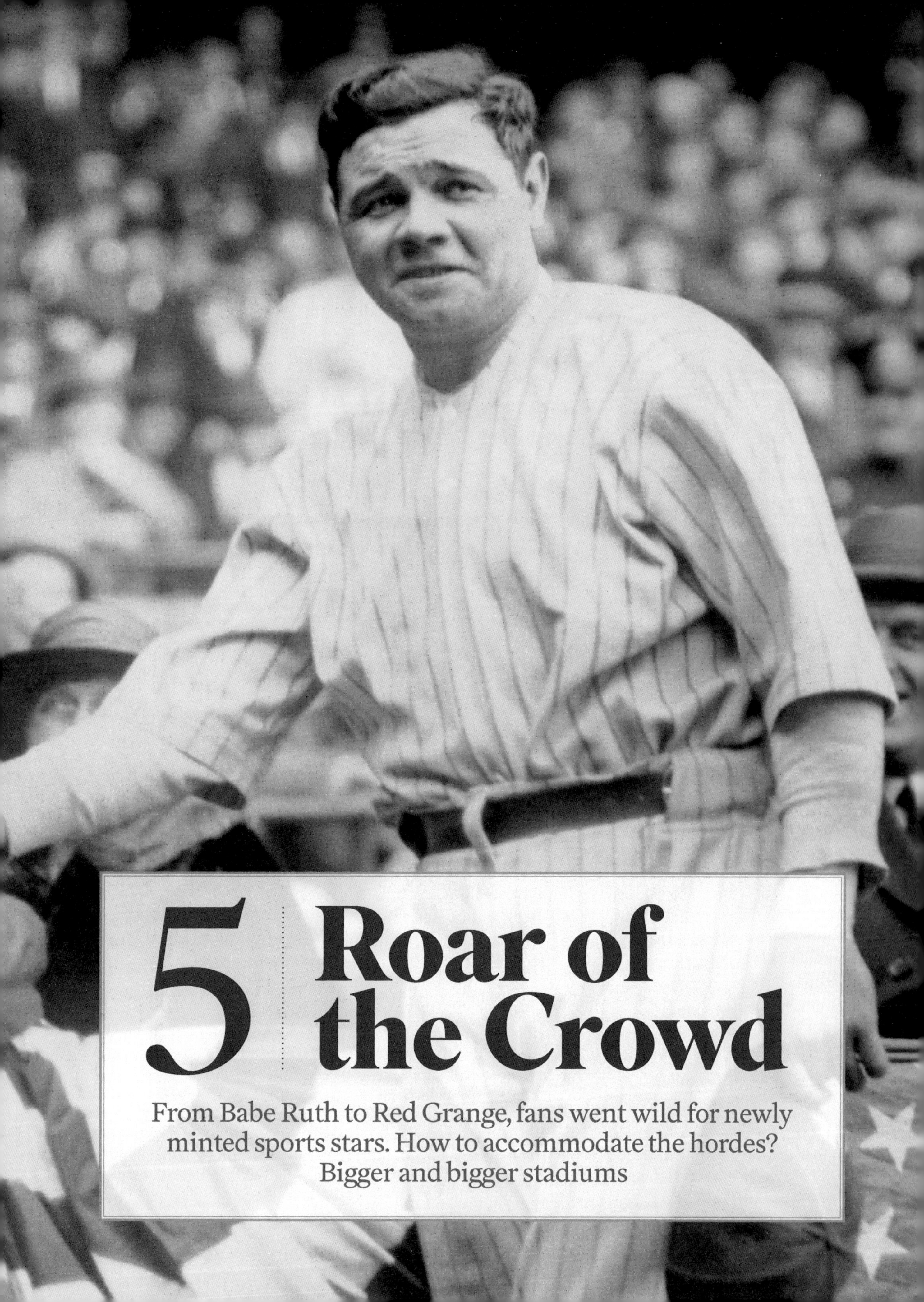

5 Roar of the Crowd

From Babe Ruth to Red Grange, fans went wild for newly minted sports stars. How to accommodate the hordes? Bigger and bigger stadiums

MASS MEDIA Attendance at venues like Brooklyn's Ebbets Field (right) was enhanced by the growth of media coverage (below).

A Golden Age

The stars aligned in the world of sports coverage. As new media fawned over athletes, they created heroes and fans. That meant more viewers and higher attendance

Until the 1920s, spectator sports were mostly a local affair. Followers of college football, the most popular sport of the era, kept tabs on regionally based conferences, not teams and players from other areas of the country. The same went for baseball: Even as the World Series gained attention, few fans had the chance to see live games, with stars like Honus Wagner of Pittsburgh and Ty Cobb of Detroit. Hockey and basketball were barely a blip on the national radar, and the National Football League had not yet been born. For many, professional sports had the aura of the unsavory—a reputation reinforced by the Black Sox scandal of 1919, when several members of the Chicago White Sox accepted bribes to throw the World Series in favor of the Cincinnati Reds. Only boxing and horse racing came close to generating a national following.

But the advent of radio and a boom in newspaper

GATES 21 & 22
FIELD STAND
ADM $2.00
TAX 20¢
TOTAL 2.20

"I'd give a year of my life if I can hit a home run in the first game in this new park."
—BABE RUTH, APRIL 1923

BOXING BOOM Jack Dempsey's 1921 bout against Georges Carpentier at Boyle's Thirty Acres in Jersey City, N.J., drew more than 100,000 fans. Dempsey (below, at left) knocked Carpentier out in the fourth round.

coverage changed these dynamics. Suddenly, fans could listen to college football and professional baseball games from all over the country and thrill to their teams' accomplishments. Big-name athletes were covered in newspapers and magazines and even featured in movie-house newsreels. Soon there were three radio networks broadcasting college football games every Saturday and five newsreel companies covering the sport. The slugger Babe Ruth, halfback Red Grange and boxing champ Jack Dempsey were just a few of the figures who became heroes to the masses. When Thoroughbred Man o' War faced off against Triple Crown winner Sir Barton in 1920, a camera crew caught them right out of the starting gate, marking the first time an entire horse race was visually recorded.

All the media attention produced record crowds. A pair of heavyweight fights between Jack Dempsey and Gene Tunney drew more than 100,000 spectators apiece. Yankee Stadium, with Babe Ruth as the marquee attraction, pulled more than 1 million fans through the turnstiles in each of its first five seasons, a record for professional baseball. Wrigley Field, home of the Chicago Cubs, attracted similar hordes, which thrilled to the exploits of power hitter Hack Wilson. In 1927, an estimated 120,000 to 130,000 college-football boosters turned out to watch Notre Dame defeat the University of Southern California. Two years later, the audience for a rematch was slightly smaller, at just 113,000, but Notre Dame wouldn't play in front of such a large crowd again until 2011. ■

If You Build It, They Will Come

As crowds for college and pro sports swelled, teams went on a stadium-building spree

MICHIGAN STADIUM
University of Michigan

At its peak, Ferry Field, where the Wolverines played originally, could accommodate just 42,000 fans. In 1927 the team moved to Michigan Stadium, which today can hold in excess of 107,000 and is nicknamed the Big House.

OPENED: 1927
ORIGINAL CAPACITY: 72,000
COST: $950,000
FUN FACT: In 1930, Michigan became the first stadium to install electronic scoreboards to keep the official time of the game.

LOS ANGELES COLISEUM
University of Southern California

The Coliseum, next door to the former Los Angeles Memorial Sports Arena (demolished in 2016), is the longtime home of the USC Trojans. The success of the two venues encouraged the migration of professional sports teams to California, including the Rams, the Dodgers and the Lakers.

OPENED: 1923
ORIGINAL CAPACITY: 75,144
COST: $955,000
FUN FACT: In 1973, daredevil Evel Knievel used his motorcycle to sail over 50 cars stacked in the middle of the Coliseum. (The exact distance of the jump is unknown.)

OHIO STADIUM
Ohio State University

When Ohio Field, opened in 1898, could no longer squeeze in the multitudes who wanted to see Buckeye games, Ohio State ordered up Ohio Stadium, with triple the seating. That might seem like overreach—it was two decades before the facility was filled to capacity on a regular basis—but the stadium has since been expanded to accommodate almost 105,000.

OPENED: 1922
ORIGINAL CAPACITY: 66,210
COST: $1.34 million
FUN FACT: The Olentangy River had to be rerouted to enable the stadium to be built.

MEMORIAL STADIUM
University of California, Berkeley

Like the Coliseum in Los Angeles, Memorial Stadium was officially commissioned as a tribute to Californians who were killed in World War I. Another factor: Berkeley wanted to keep up with rival Stanford University, which had opened a new 60,000-seat stadium in 1921.

OPENED: 1923
ORIGINAL CAPACITY: 72,609
COST: $1.4 million
FUN FACT: Just as in the '20s, a hill on the east side of the stadium attracts fans hoping to see the game for free, earning it the name Tightwad Hill.

YANKEE STADIUM
New York Yankees

Many of the classic baseball stadiums, including Fenway Park and Wrigley Field, opened between 1910 and 1920. The biggest of them all, Yankee Stadium, was a relative latecomer. Known as the House That Ruth Built in tribute to the team's most popular star, the stadium was an instant hit.

OPENED: 1923
ORIGINAL CAPACITY: 57,000
COST: $2.4 million
FUN FACT: Estimates vary, but at least 60,000 fans, the most in baseball history at the time, showed up for opening day in the new stadium. Babe Ruth, of course, hit the game's first (and only) home run in a 4–1 victory over, you guessed it, the Boston Red Sox.

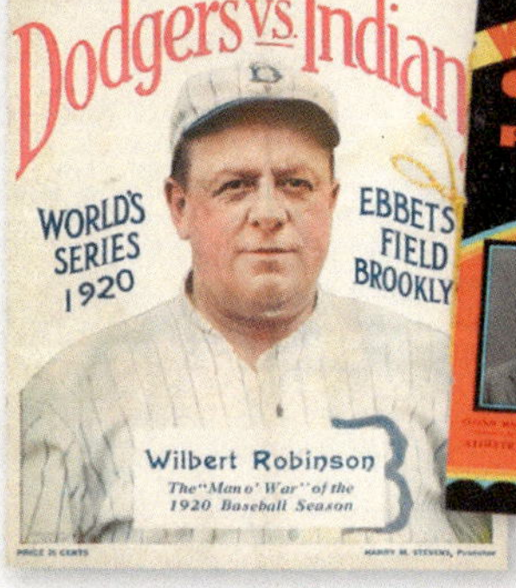

"What a football player, this man Red Grange. He is melody and symphony. He is crashing sound. He is brute force."
—DAMON RUNYON, 1924

A Gallery of Greats

The first true sports superstars emerged in the 1920s

Red Grange

A key player in college, Grange lent instant credibility to the fledgling National Football League

To this day, Red Grange (right), a bruising but elusive running back, is considered one of football's most influential players. He set the tone for his career in his very first varsity game, for the University of Illinois, when he scored three touchdowns on runs of 35 yards, 65 yards and 12 yards against Nebraska. Later in the season, Grange helped Illinois achieve its first victory ever against the University of Iowa, bulldozing his way into the end zone from the two-yard line on the game's critical drive.

And then there was Grange's artistry in the 1924 face-off against Michigan, considered by some the single greatest performance in college football history. He returned the opening kickoff 95 yards for a touchdown, followed that with a 67-yard touchdown run on Illinois's first play from scrimmage, then dashed his way through the Michigan defense on touchdown runs of 54 and 44 yards. (All this in the first 12 minutes of the game.) Later Grange ran for a fifth score and threw a touchdown pass for a sixth en route to a 39–14 shellacking of the Wolverines. "What a football player, this man Red Grange," Damon Runyon wrote at the time. "He is melody and symphony. He is crashing sound. He is brute force."

By the time Grange's college career neared its end in 1925, the newly founded NFL desperately needed a star to establish its credibility. More than 20 league teams had folded over a four-year period, and attendance was sparse. In some cases, fewer than 100 spectators showed up on game days. The league saw a solution in Grange, and he was courted by several teams, most notably the Rochester Jeffersons and the Chicago Bears. Rochester offered Grange $5,000 a game, but Chicago beat it by promising him $3,000 per game plus a significant share of the gate to play in a 19-game, 67-day, mostly exhibition tour.

The lure of so much easy and quick cash proved irresistible. Grange dropped out of Illinois and joined the barnstorming tour, which kicked off on Thanksgiving Day in 1925. It was an almost immediate success, drawing an average of 10,000 fans per game. For the December contest between the Bears and the New York Giants in the Polo Grounds in New York City, a whopping 65,000 spectators showed up. Babe Ruth was there, as were more than 100 sportswriters. In the space of barely two months, Grange had rescued the NFL and earned a cool $100,000.

Grange never achieved the same level of success in the pros as he had in college, however. A knee injury in 1927 seriously limited his speed and agility. But he became a solid straight-ahead runner and a gifted defensive back. In the 1933 title against the Giants, Grange made a game-saving tackle near his own goal line as time expired to preserve Chicago's 23–21 victory. ■

Jack Dempsey

He pummeled his opponents in the ring but won fans outside it with his humble, approachable style

Jack Dempsey (below) grew up poor, moving with his itinerant parents from Colorado to West Virginia and then to Utah before dropping out of school and leaving home at 16. Traveling underneath trains and sleeping in "hobo" camps, Dempsey supported himself with odd jobs and occasionally by striding into saloons and challenging willing barflies to a bare-knuckle match. After goading patrons into placing bets, Dempsey almost always emerged the victor—and with a little additional cash in his pocket.

Once Dempsey turned pro, he established himself as a powerful though not very artistic fighter. He dispatched most of his opponents with knockouts, frequently in the early rounds, and the press covered his every move with rapt attention. While fans flocked in droves to Dempsey's fights, they did not really take the new champion to their hearts until he lost the title in 1926 to the more skillful Gene Tunney. Humble in defeat, Dempsey told his wife, "Honey, I forgot to duck." When Tunney and Dempsey fought again in Chicago in 1927, 105,000 fans packed Soldier Field. Some 50 million more listened to Graham McNamee's radio broadcast.

Dempsey knocked Tunney down in the seventh round, but he made a critical mistake when he failed to move to a neutral corner as the new rules prescribed. The slipup gave Tunney time to recover, and he came back to win the bout in a decision. Dempsey supporters argued that he would have won had Tunney not been granted the extra time, a controversy that has gone down in boxing annals as the "long count."

Dempsey was a gracious loser, calling Tunney a great champion, but soon after the loss he retired and opened a restaurant in New York City. He also made several unsuccessful forays into movies and onto the Broadway stage, generally appearing opposite one of his first two wives (of four). Mostly he was known for being a gentleman and always stopping for fans on the street or in his restaurant. As described by legendary sports columnist Red Smith in Dempsey's 1983 obituary in the *New York Times*: "He was warm and generous, a free spender when he had it and a soft touch for anybody down on his luck."

Babe Ruth

The biggest star of them all revolutionized baseball by hitting a ton of towering home runs

And then there was the Babe, the irrepressible man-child. Sold by the Boston Red Sox to the New York Yankees for $100,000 in January 1920, Ruth (right) went on an offensive tear that established the home run as baseball's most potent offensive weapon. In his first season wearing pinstripes, Ruth led the major leagues in home runs (54), runs batted in (135), runs (158), walks (150), on-base percentage (.532) and slugging percentage (.847). His 54 home runs were more than the total of any other *team* in the league.

Off the field, Ruth cast almost as massive a shadow. He was loud, brash and larger than life, and the tales of his relentless womanizing were well known, though largely unreported by a worshipful press. One story described him being pursued through a train by an angry woman with a knife, upset by her discovery that she was not Ruth's only paramour. Another claimed that Ruth was chased, nearly naked, out of a Detroit hotel by an angry husband wielding a gun.

This boorish behavior was somewhat offset by his genuine affection for his fans, particularly the

thousands of kids who worshipped him. His most famous act of kindness came during the 1926 World Series. The exact details are a bit hazy, but the gist is that after hearing about an ailing young fan, Johnny Sylvester, Ruth sent the boy a package with two autographed baseballs to cheer him up. He also included a note promising that "I'll hit a homer for you on Wednesday." In fact, Ruth knocked out three in a 10–5 Yankee win in Series Game 4.

Ruth's success made him an extremely valuable commodity, and he was well aware of it. When word leaked out that Ruth was negotiating a salary of $80,000 for himself in 1930, he was asked whether he thought it appropriate that he should be paid $5,000 more than the president of the United States. "What the hell has Hoover got to do with it?" was Ruth's typically bold response. "Besides, I had a better year than he did."

Bobby Jones

The only man to win golf's Grand Slam also pioneered its most legendary event: the Masters

Of all the celebrated golfers of the 1920s, none was more famous than Bobby Jones (left), the gentlemanly Georgian who won 13 major championships (still the third most in golf history) from 1923 to 1930.

A child prodigy, Jones shot an 80 at age 11 at Atlanta's East Lake Country Club. Yet he had an Achilles' heel. Prone to extreme performance anxiety, Jones sometimes vomited before tournaments. He also struggled with mood swings through his teenage years, and he frequently threw his clubs in anger after making a bad shot. In 1921, during the third round of the British Open, the 19-year-old Jones walked off St. Andrews's 11th hole after failing to get out of a bunker. It took time, but eventually he mastered his temper and developed a more consistent game.

In 1930, Jones became the only player to win golf's Grand Slam, traveling across the pond to win the British Amateur and British Open, then returning home to capture the U.S. Amateur and U.S. Open. He surprised the world by retiring at the top of his game at 28, knowing his future was already secure—he had passed the Georgia bar exam and would be able to move smoothly into his career as a lawyer with his father's firm in Atlanta.

Jones was hardly through with golf, however. In 1930, looking to build a course where he might play in peace, he purchased property in Augusta, Ga. The resulting course, codesigned with Alister MacKenzie, became America's most celebrated club: Augusta National, which officially opened in 1933. One year later, the first Masters Tournament was played at the club, and the event has remained there ever since.

Man o' War

Many experts still consider the massive colt the greatest Thoroughbred in racing history

The decade also produced Man o' War (above), perhaps the most talented horse ever to set hoof on an American track. A huge fan favorite, the horse was originally named "My Man o' War" by a wife in honor of her husband, who was fighting in World War I (the "My" was later dropped). This was an enormous beast. Man o' War tipped the scales at 1,150 pounds and had a gargantuan stride (25 to 28 feet) and an appetite to match, allegedly consuming 12 quarts of oats a day.

In 1919 and 1920, Man o' War won 20 of his 21 starts, including the last two legs of the Triple Crown in 1920, the Preakness and Belmont Stakes—the latter by 20 lengths while demolishing the track record by more than three seconds. His most famous race may have been his last, at Kenilworth Park in Windsor, Ontario, where Man o' War handily defeated Sir Barton, who had became horse racing's first Triple Crown winner in 1919.

To this day, experts argue about whether Man o' War or 1973 Triple Crown winner Secretariat is the greatest of all time. The jury is still out, but Man o' War was the clear champion in the breeding shed, siring more than 64 Stakes winners and champions, including War Admiral, who won the Triple Crown in 1937. ■

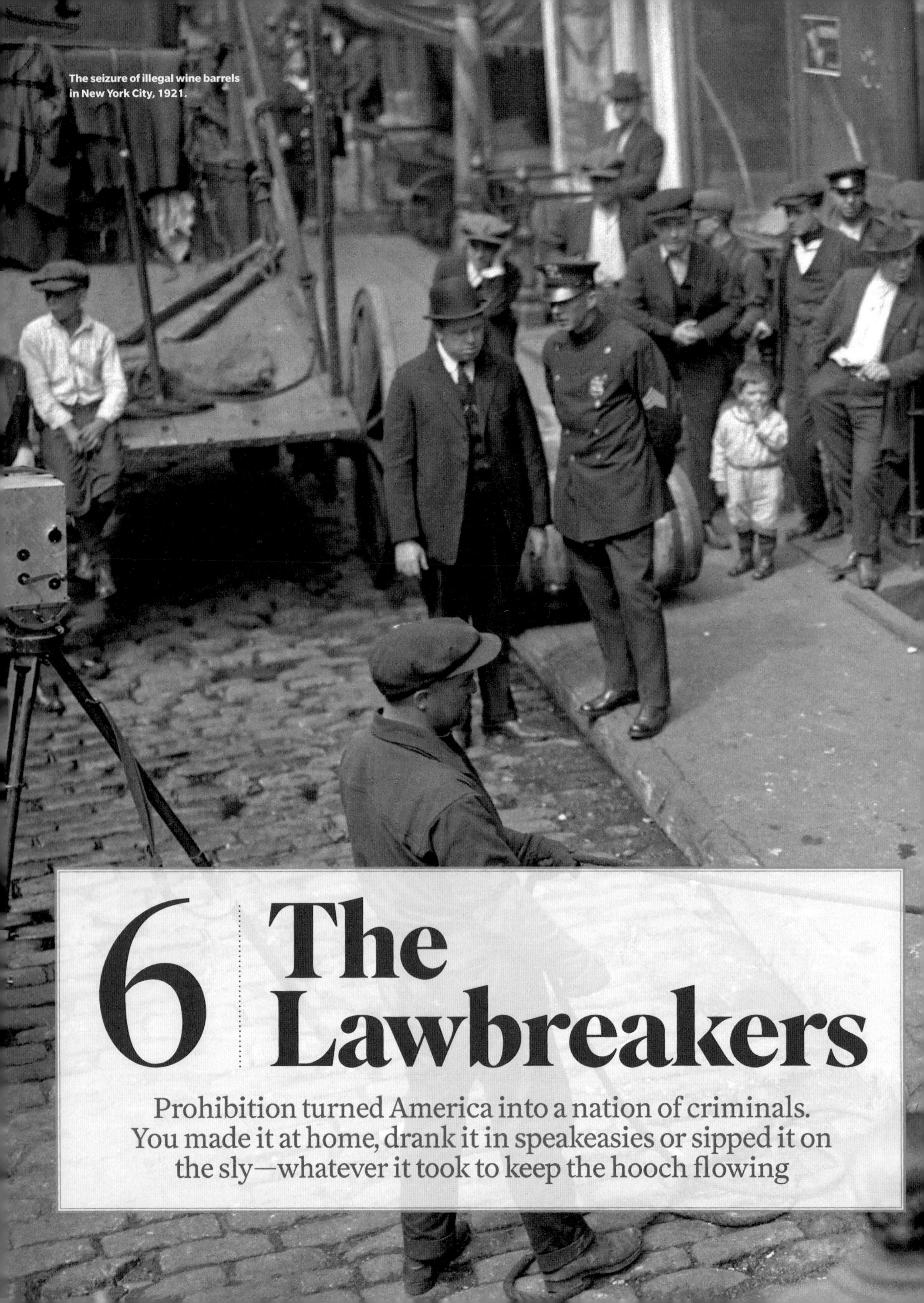

The seizure of illegal wine barrels in New York City, 1921.

6 The Lawbreakers

Prohibition turned America into a nation of criminals. You made it at home, drank it in speakeasies or sipped it on the sly—whatever it took to keep the hooch flowing

UNSTOPPABLE The authorities put on a good show, arresting flamboyant speakeasy operators like Texas Guinan (right) and pouring liquor down the drain (below), but all the efforts amounted to very little. Guinan was soon back in business, and the booze kept flowing freely.

A Failed Experiment

The cops and the politicians took bribes to look the other way while the public happily skirted the law. Prohibition never had a chance

The 1920s were barely two weeks old when the United States embarked on one of the maddest experiments of a mad decade. On January 16, the 18th Amendment became law, making liquor, beer and wine illegal throughout the country. The legislation, passed at the urging of religious temperance groups, was an abysmal failure pretty much from the start. Not only did Americans continue to make, barter and hold on to alcohol, but many drank even more of it. Women, who in the past had never been allowed in bars, trooped into the new, secret saloons, where they tried out the latest fad—mixed drinks, known as cocktails.

The black market boomed. By 1925, there were thought to be 100,000 speakeasies in New York City alone. The famous saloon owner Texas Guinan—who greeted her patrons with a sassy "Hello, sucker!"—was said to have taken in $700,000 in a 10-month period. Moonshining became big business. So did smuggling. Hundreds of ships were anchored three miles off the

"Prohibition has made nothing but trouble—trouble for all of us."

—AL CAPONE, 1932

KNOCK, KNOCK
Speakeasies offered a whiff of glamorous transgression.

Atlantic Coast, in a line from Maine to Florida, dispensing liquor to anyone who chose to come out and get it.

Enforcement of Prohibition was tepid at best, led by an overworked group of just 1,550 federal agents. Sometimes they got help from local and state authorities, but often the officials themselves were part of the problem. They either looked the other way or extorted bribes from bootleggers so they could stay in business. One New York speakeasy owner estimated it cost him $1,370 a month to operate—$400 of which was paid out to the feds, police and district attorneys. His beat cop got another $40 to turn his back whenever beer was delivered. In Texas, just a few months after the start of Prohibition, an operating still was discovered on the farm of Senator Morris Sheppard, one of the authors of the 18th Amendment. It was turning out 130 gallons of whiskey a day. ■

BEATING THE SYSTEM

Americans found ingenious methods to conceal their illegal liquor, and ways to produce it too

Getting around Prohibition became a kind of parlor game for drinkers all over the nation. Some flouted the law simply by concealing their booze in hip flasks, beneath garter belts or in hiding places like canes, false books and coconut shells. Others filled hot-water bottles and strung them on neck cords to hang under their clothes. There were those who siphoned their hooch into garden hoses wrapped around their waists or who hid it under babies perched in their strollers. One man was caught crossing the International Bridge in Buffalo, N.Y., carrying two boxes of eggs, every one of which had been drained and refilled with liquor.

Lots of drinkers simply made their own booze at home. For six or seven dollars, consumers could buy a portable still from almost any hardware store. California winemakers sold Vine-Glo, a grape-juice product that was quite legal but when put in the cellar and nursed for 60 days turned into wine that was 15 percent alcohol. Unfortunately, the brew-it-yourself varieties were often poisonous and sometimes even lethal because the recipes included industrial alcohol. As many as 10,000 people died because of the DIY concoctions. Some of those deaths, shockingly enough, resulted from a federal program to discourage the use of industrial alcohol by making it even more toxic than it already was.

HIDING THE HOOCH Some drinkers carried their booze in contraptions like this bottle-toting vest, which could be worn under an overcoat.

GANG WARFARE Cops loaded the body of Dean O'Banion into a police wagon (right) in 1924. The mobster's death ignited a five-year internecine war with the gang headed by Al Capone (below). O'Banion's funeral allegedly cost $100,000 and was attended by 10,000 people.

Mob Rule

Prohibition offered organized crime the chance to make a lot of money by giving the public precisely what it wanted: booze, and plenty of it

Of all the evils to come out of Prohibition, the worst was the unbridled growth of big-time organized crime. Gangsters were nothing new. For years, they had been running saloons, brothels and gambling joints and doing dirty work for employers and workers alike in labor disputes. But when the Mob got into bootlegging, the violent turf wars, intimidation tactics and murderous rampages that followed were like nothing the U.S. had ever seen.

The most famous and cold-blooded gangster of all, of course, was Chicago's Al Capone. With 700 men to do his bidding, Capone dominated the East Coast bootlegging business from Canada to Florida, and before the end of the decade, he controlled 10,000 speakeasies. His ruthlessness was legend. Capone quashed rival gangs who rose up to challenge him, and gang murders in Chicago spiked during Prohibition, with more than 400 members killed a year.

Capone's biggest rival was an Irish-American gang run by the flamboyant florist Dean O'Banion. In late 1924, after O'Banion insulted another mobster in a

BLOODY THURSDAY Graphic photographs of the St. Valentine's Day Massacre like the one below outraged the public and led to a far more serious effort to address the scourge of organized crime. Capone was arrested in 1929 and spent almost all of the next 13 years in prison. He died in 1947.

heated phone call, he was murdered as he clipped chrysanthemums in his flower shop. The hit ignited a bloody five-year war that culminated with Capone allegedly signing off on the infamous St. Valentine's Day Massacre of 1929. Four of Capone's men, two of them posing as police officers, entered a warehouse, lined up seven O'Banion gang members and associates and mowed them down with Thompson submachine guns. O'Banion boss Bugsy Moran was not present, though historians have speculated that the killers, mistaking Moran for a lieutenant with similar features, believed he was.

A few months later, two hit men thought to have been involved in the massacre were found dead in Hammond, Ind. Lore has it that Capone beat them to death with a baseball bat after learning that they intended to turn on him. The episode was echoed in *The Untouchables,* a 1987 gangster thriller with Robert De Niro as Capone. In it, De Niro pulls out a bat at a dinner party and beats one of his men to death.

The brutality of the St. Valentine's Day Massacre and its aftermath shocked even longtime Chicago observers. The killings led to a series of efforts to bring organized crime under control, but nothing did more to curb the era's violence than the end of Prohibition in 1933. ■

TWIN KILLING **Gaertner (above) and Annan (inset) were both found not guilty in sensational trials that gripped the nation with lurid tales of jealousy, sex and murder.**

Velma and Roxie for Real

A pair of celebrated murders captured the public imagination and inspired the hit musical Chicago

IT WAS the oddest of trends: in the violent Chicago of the 1920s, a spate of women killed their husbands or lovers, only to be acquitted by all-male juries who seemed to believe that females were incapable of murder. Two of the most famous perpetrators were the cabaret singer Belva Gaertner and Beulah Annan, who was celebrated for her beauty. The women's trials were covered in great detail by *Chicago Tribune* reporter Maurine Watkins, whose stories made it clear that justice had not been served. Alas, instead of provoking outrage, Watkins's stories served only to arouse widespread popular support for the pair, who became media celebrities.

A possessive lover, the thrice-divorced Gaertner shot her younger boyfriend, Walter Law, in her car when he threatened to leave her. Law's body was discovered in the vehicle next to an empty gin bottle and a gun with three rounds missing, and Gaertner was later found in her home in blood-covered clothes. The defense argued that Law committed suicide and Gaertner had fled in a panic. The jury bought it, in spite of the three bullets. Case closed.

Annan, whose victim was a man named Harry Kalstedt, had even more difficult circumstances to explain. She first shot Kalstedt point-blank in the back, then sat in her apartment listening to a foxtrot song called "Hula Lou" over and over as her lover died before her. Through the investigation and trial, Annan changed her story several times, finally settling on an account in which she and Kalstedt struggled for the gun and he was shot by accident. How Kalstedt was shot in the back remained a mystery. No one was at all surprised by the verdict. Not guilty.

Disgusted with Chicago-style justice, Watkins moved to New York soon after the trials and wrote a play called *Chicago* about the two women. Beulah became Roxie Hart and Belva became Velma Kelly, later immortalized in the Bob Fosse musical of the same name (1975) and finally in the hit movie (2002) starring Catherine Zeta-Jones and Renée Zellweger in the two lead roles.

The stories of Belva and Beulah were just two of the juicy tales that filled the pages of the tabloids, a new breed of publication specializing in all things sensational. Readers were seduced by lurid headlines and a new set of catchphrases—love nests, torch murderers, sugar daddies—that hinted at the story's likely content. Crime was the most frequent topic, though sex certainly sold as well, and if the two could be combined, you had a guaranteed hit story.

Among the popular tabloid tales: the murder trials of beautiful Queens, N.Y., housewife Ruth Snyder and her married lover, Henry Judd Gray, who were convicted of killing Snyder's husband for the insurance policy. Then there were the faked kidnapping of flamboyant evangelist Aimee Semple McPherson and the "thrill" killing of 14-year-old Bobby Franks by a pair of college students, Nathan Leopold and Richard Loeb. Most titillating of all: the failed marriage of "Daddy," a 51-year-old real estate mogul named Edward Browning, and "Peaches," his 15-year-old wife, the actress Frances Browning. Competing stories from the pair during their divorce kept readers transfixed for days.

Edmund Burns and Norma Shearer being filmed in *Broadway After Dark*, 1924.

7 The Dream Factory

The studio system took hold, and the movie industry went from silent films to talkies, hooking audiences

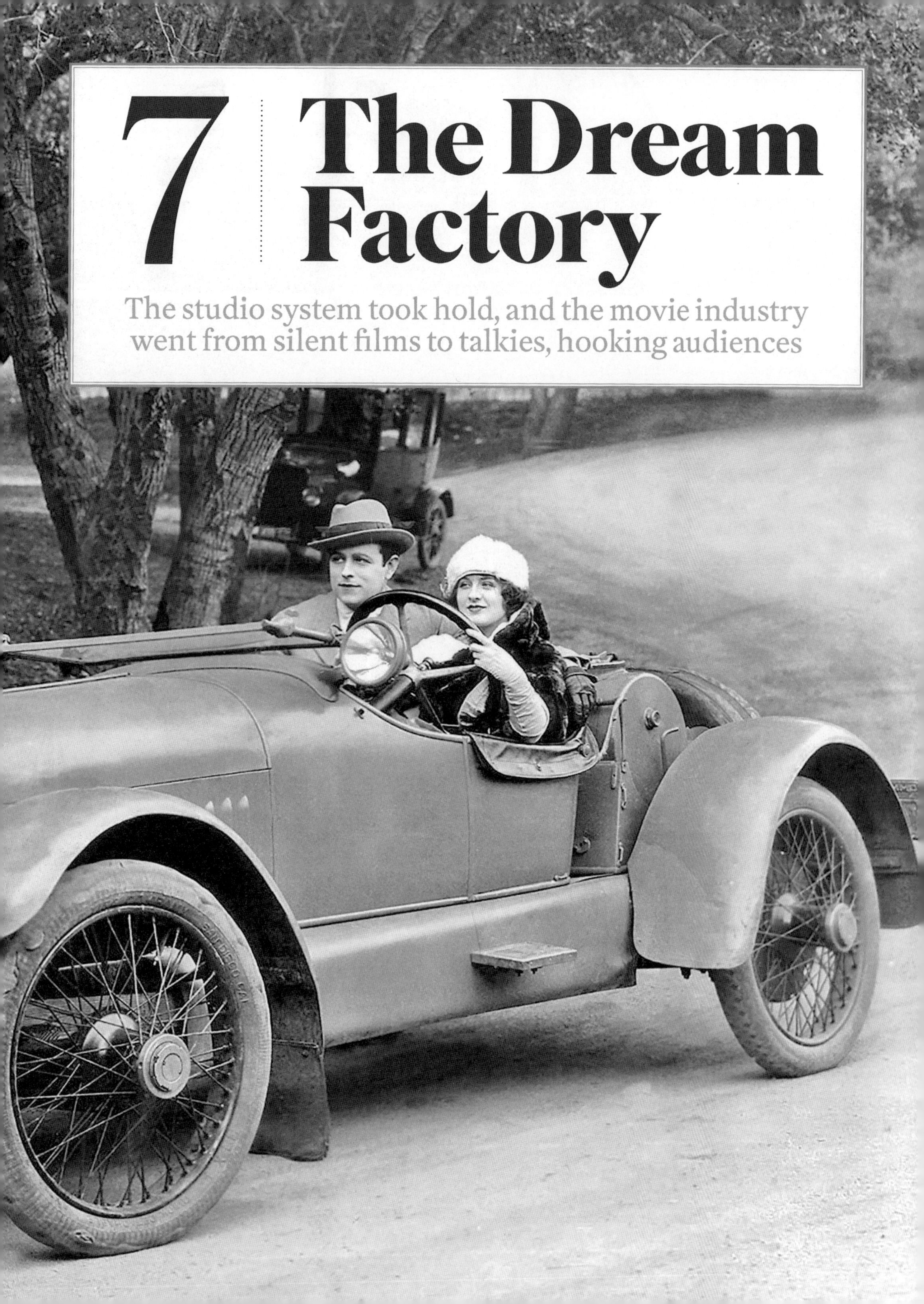

CINEMATIC MAGIC
In *The Temptress* (1926), Greta Garbo's character, Elena (right), drove her many suitors mad, including Manuel, played by Antonio Moreno. The MGM lion (below), with his famous roar, was filmed in 1928.

Silver Screen, Box-Office Gold

Making movies was both art and commerce. Studio executives learned to streamline the system to boost the bottom line

The movies were already popular—some 35 million Americans went to the cinema at least once a week in 1920. But as the Hollywood studio system became established, that number increased dramatically, to 50 million by 1925, and by decade's end to a staggering 70 million out of a total population of 122 million.

That growth was driven, in part, by the huge volume of films being produced—close to 800 a year for much of the decade (compared with some 500 today). Five studios dominated: MGM, Paramount Pictures, RKO, Warner Bros. and 20th Century Fox. Each had its own style, along with its own actors and directors, which guaranteed predictable quality and profitable formulas. Among the most successful were westerns, slapstick comedies, musicals, adventure/swashbucklers and romances.

As leading actors became box-office draws, studio heads, who had long resisted paying actors large salaries, realized the value of stars. If an actress like Lillian Gish developed a fan base and as a result helped sell

POMP AND PUBLICITY Loew's Kings Theatre in Brooklyn originally opened in 1929 and closed in 1977, but it was restored and reopened in 2015 (right). The Hollywood publicity apparatus promoted stars like Clara Bow (below) and Charlie Chaplin (bottom).

more tickets, she might really be worth the $400,000 she was allegedly getting in 1926. Studio executives and their publicity men began to nurture and promote popular talent. The booming business attracted hopefuls from around the country and indeed the world. Directors like Ernst Lubitsch, Alfred Hitchcock and Jean Renoir flocked to Hollywood from Europe, accompanied by actors like Rudolph Valentino, Greta Garbo, Charlie Chaplin and Ronald Colman.

Finally, Hollywood was revolutionized by the advent of synchronous sound movies, more popularly known as the talkies. Early films had included bits of dialogue on film and in singing sequences, but words were not part of the dramatic unfolding of the plot. That changed the moment in 1927 that Al Jolson uttered the first line of dialogue in *The Jazz Singer*—"Wait a minute, wait a minute. You ain't heard nothin' yet!" Hollywood was about to undergo a sea change. For a few, the innovation spelled the end of a promising career. But for most, particularly those who brought genuine dramatic skill to their work, the introduction of sound and dialogue offered a new means to touch the hearts of their audiences. ■

Movie Palaces

Studios lured audiences with enormous, lavish theaters

AS THE FILMS themselves became more exciting, so did outings to the movie houses where they were shown. Flush with cash, studios sought to outdo one another, buying and upgrading scores of independent venues, as well as building lavish theaters, many of them truly deserving of the title "movie palaces." These were edifices as huge as the celluloid dreams they offered. The truly mammoth ones, such as the Roxy in New York and the Fox in Detroit, seated some 5,000 people. New York's Capitol Theater, holding 5,300, was so cavernous that a movie magazine remarked, "The mezzanine floor looks as if it had been designed for eight-day bicycle races."

The new theaters created a fantasy environment where audiences could escape quotidian life. Their visual styles were wildly exotic and ranged from French baroque and Aztec to Italian Renaissance and, after the discovery of King Tut's tomb in 1922, Egyptian Revival. Screens were hidden behind lush, plush velvet curtains that rose dramatically as the show began, and uniformed ushers and well-stocked concession stands became de rigueur features.

ENDURING STARS Pickford and Fairbanks were always friendly with the press and remained popular even as their movie careers began to fade with the rise of the talkies.

Hollywood Royalty

She was the dewy-eyed innocent, he the heroic swashbuckler. Together, Mary Pickford and Douglas Fairbanks became the preeminent movie stars of the silent era

The decade produced a host of stars, but none shone more brightly than Mary Pickford and Douglas Fairbanks, whose marriage in 1920 established them at the outset as the Queen and King of Hollywood.

Gladys Louise Smith was born in Toronto in 1892 into a family of limited means. Her alcoholic father died when she was 6, and Smith took up acting to help support her mother and two siblings. After winning a series of theatrical roles, the young actress made her way to Broadway, where producer David Belasco recommended that she change her name. Smith adopted Pickford from her mother's side of the family and Mary just because she liked it.

As Pickford approached her late teens, parts began to dry up; casting directors considered her too old to take the parts of children and still too young for romantic leads. In desperation, Pickford turned to the new and largely unproven medium of film. At the time, director D.W. Griffith, with his movie company Biograph, was still based in New York, and soon Pickford and Griffith were collaborating on the pioneering silent films that catapulted her into the limelight.

Pickford developed an intimate style for the silver screen that became her trademark. She learned to express emotions with her eyes and to emote naturally in front of the camera. After appearing in a series of hits for producer Adolph Zukor, Pickford earned the nickname "America's Sweetheart." In 1915 she was seen globally by an estimated 12 million people a day.

Fairbanks, meanwhile, achieved similar success on the male side of the ledger. Born in 1883 in Denver, Fairbanks, like Pickford, was young—only 5 years old—when his alcoholic father abandoned the family, and by the time he was 11, Fairbanks had begun his stage career. He eventually landed roles on Broadway and then migrated to film. He was suave, handsome and exceptionally athletic, qualities that made him the perfect actor to pioneer the new adventure/swashbuckler genre. *The Mark of Zorro* (1920), *The Three Musketeers* (1921) and *Robin Hood* (1922), all with Fairbanks in the lead, were enormously popular, and they established Fairbanks as the most bankable male star of the day.

Fairbanks and Pickford first met in 1916 and, by all accounts, fell in love immediately. Both were in unhappy marriages and feared that a public affair would damage their careers, so they kept their relationship hidden. Finally, in 1920, they each divorced their spouses and were married. Contrary to the couple's fears, they were warmly embraced by fans, who thrilled to every detail the press could glean from their life together. Of particular interest was the 18-acre palatial estate, dubbed Pickfair by the media, that Fairbanks had built for his wife in Beverly Hills. Alas, the fairy tale faltered. Pickford did not take to the talkies and made her last film appearance in 1933. Fairbanks's career languished too—he was 44 by the time sound took over in 1927. The couple divorced in 1936.

"Life is a tragedy when seen in close-up, but a comedy in long-shot."
—CHARLIE CHAPLIN

Glittering Firmament

The Little Tramp. The It Girl. And the Face

Charlie Chaplin

The Little Tramp, beloved by audiences, delivered comedy and pathos, laughter and tears

Comic actors Harold Lloyd and Buster Keaton were both brilliant, as were the Marx Brothers, who delighted audiences with their unique brand of screwball satire. But the undisputed comic genius of the 1920s and beyond was British-born Charlie Chaplin (right).

Chaplin was a perfectionist who wrote, directed, produced, edited and starred in all his movies; he even composed the music for many of them. The result was a series of masterpieces, including *The Gold Rush* (1925), *The Circus* (1928), *City Lights* (1931) and *Modern Times* (1936). The star's recurring character, the Little Tramp, combined comedy and pathos so poignantly that audience members were moved to laugh and cry almost simultaneously.

Some did not view Chaplin so positively. He was hounded by the FBI during the 1940s for alleged Communist sympathies. He was also the victim of a spurious paternity suit and widely criticized for his marriage in 1943 to Oona O'Neill, 36 years his junior. Exhausted by the negative attention, Chaplin finally left the country in 1952 and did not return until 1972, when he traveled to Los Angeles to accept an honorary Academy Award. The star-studded audience gave him a 12-minute standing ovation, the longest in the history of the Academy Awards.

Greta Garbo

An exotic beauty won acclaim for her talent, sophistication and, mostly, her silence

Actress Greta Garbo (above) was discovered in Sweden and brought to the U.S. in 1925 by MGM boss Louis B. Mayer. But it was a young studio producer, Irving Thalberg, who cast Garbo in her first American film, *Torrent*, and who crafted the image that she would project for much of her early career: worldly wise, sophisticated and possessed of an undeniable and highly distinctive beauty. By the time of Garbo's third picture, *Flesh and the Devil* (1926)—her first of four opposite heartthrob John Gilbert—she was one of the studio's biggest stars. The shift to talking pictures only increased her allure, and her first speaking feature, *Anna Christie* (1930), was hyped with the come-on "Garbo talks!" The talented actress was nominated for four Academy Awards before she retired from acting in 1941 at just 36 years old.

In the decades that followed, Garbo shunned publicity and declined to give interviews. Although she never married or had children, there were tales of affairs, including an admitted romance with Gilbert, and many more rumored with various men and women in her orbit. Garbo maintained a loyal cadre of intimates throughout her life, including Thalberg and his wife, actress Norma Shearer, and Thalberg's death at the age of just 37 in 1936 hit her hard. She passed away in 1990, silent to the end.

Rudolph Valentino

A small-time actor's career was launched after he danced a seductive tango in a 1921 hit

Rudolph Valentino (below) immigrated to the U.S. from his native Italy in 1913 at age 18. He survived in the early years by performing a variety of odd jobs, eventually entering show business as a nightclub dancer. In 1917 he went to Hollywood to try his hand at acting but was able to land only small roles, usually as a bad guy. All that changed when Valentino was cast as one of the leads in *The Four Horsemen of the Apocalypse* in 1921. From his first scene in the movie, in which Valentino dances a seductive tango, it was evident that studio executives had missed a quality the outrageously handsome actor possessed in abundance: sex appeal. Valentino became an instant sensation, swooned over by a horde of fans.

Over the next five years, Valentino defined the Latin lover persona that would become a stock Hollywood character for decades to come. The star's reign was sadly brief; he died from peritonitis in 1926. Thousands of grief-stricken well-wishers crowded a funeral home in New York City to view the body over three days, and services were held in both California and New York.

Clara Bow

How did the original "It Girl" earn the nickname? Not how you think

Clara Bow (below) is largely remembered as a style icon. Her short, bobbed hair, Cupid's-bow lips and athletic fashions all became flapper staples. But Bow was also a genuine movie star who appeared in a series of box-office hits, including *Mantrap* (1926) and *Wings* (1927). By some estimates, she was the top box-office draw in 1928 and 1929, and the second-leading earner in 1927. She received more than 45,000 fan letters in the single month of January 1929. She got her famous nickname, the It Girl, not, as we might expect, because she expressed the spirit of her age, but rather from one of her popular movies, *It*.

Bow stopped making films after 1933, retiring to her ranch in Nevada. Many believe that her heavy Brooklyn accent sabotaged her career as talkies took off. But the truth is that Bow found Hollywood too stressful and chose to leave because of mental-health issues, which plagued her for the rest of her life.

Lillian Gish

Gish's deal with MGM was so lucrative that she asked for a cut to pay supporting actors more

Widely considered the finest actress of the silent era, Lillian Gish (above) did more than any other performer to define the techniques that worked on film. Her trademark wistful gestures and contemplative looks offered viewers a portal into her characters' souls. Fragile and vulnerable, Gish presented the perfect persona for the delicate damsels in distress she often played.

Like so many stars of the 1920s, Gish entered show business as a child. When she was 19, her life-long friend and New York City neighbor Mary Pickford introduced her to director D.W. Griffith. Soon she was appearing in various Griffith productions, including feature-length films like the controversial *Birth of a Nation* in 1915.

Gish left Griffith in 1925 for a deal with MGM that was so lucrative that she negotiated her contract down so her supporting actors and crew could get paid more. Gish shifted her focus to the theater in the 1930s and '40s, then returned to movies and the new medium of television in the 1950s. Her final film was the 1987 drama *Whales of August*, about two elderly and incompatible sisters played by Gish and another screen legend, Bette Davis. Gish died at 99 in 1993.

Typecasting Begins

Tom Mix and Lon Chaney both found lucrative niches in the movies playing predictable roles in profitable genres

WHILE MANY of the early stars were able to work in a variety of movies, playing serious romantic leads in one film, lighthearted comic roles in the next and swashbuckling action heroes in a third, others were much more restricted. Two of the biggest names of the decade, Tom Mix (below) and Lon Chaney (right, in *The Phantom of the Opera*), became stars of their own very particular emerging genres.

Before appearing in his first western in 1910, Mix worked as a cowboy and traveled with Wild West shows, and his real-life experience showed on the screen. He was a bona fide cowboy hero and skilled horseman—his beloved Tony the Wonder Horse was almost as famous as he was—and also performed all his own stunts. By 1917, Mix was under contract with Fox, and over the next 12 years, he made an average of five films a year for the studio, many of them box-office hits. But the money Mix earned didn't last. He burned through most of it during the course of five marriages and several lavish spending sprees. When he died in an automobile accident in 1940, he had never appeared in anything but a western.

Chaney was a significantly more talented actor, but he too was largely genre-bound, creating a series of grotesque characters in horror movies, such as *The Hunchback of Notre Dame* (1923) and *The Phantom of the Opera* (1925). Even when appearing in more conventional crime or adventure movies, Chaney almost always played a complex if somewhat macabre figure with a physical defect. His performances were utterly believable and widely acclaimed for humanizing tortured souls.

"I wanted to remind people that the lowest types of humanity may have within them the capacity for supreme self-sacrifice," Chaney wrote in his autobiography. "The dwarfed, misshapen beggar of the streets may have the noblest ideals. Most of my roles since *The Hunchback* ... have carried the theme of self-sacrifice or renunciation. These are the stories which I wish to do." He died from bronchial lung cancer in 1930.

John Barrymore

Many considered him the most talented member of the famous acting clan, but his career was destroyed by alcohol

The story of John Barrymore (above) is a tragic one. He was a highly acclaimed stage actor well before he began his film career. He appeared in a series of successful silent movies—an early performance as the lead in *Dr. Jekyll and Mr. Hyde* (1920) was particularly well received—and his star only rose further with the advent of sound. By the time he appeared in *Svengali* in 1931, he was earning a hefty $150,000 per picture.

His personal life, on the other hand, was a mess. A hopeless alcoholic, Barrymore blew through his money and his four marriages, eventually losing even the ability to remember his lines. He died in 1942 of cirrhosis of the liver and kidney failure.

His actor siblings, Ethel and Lionel, did not share John's troubles. Ethel appeared in a number of memorable films but remained most committed to the stage. Lionel was a brilliant character actor—audiences today remember him most vividly as the avaricious banker Henry Potter in the Christmas classic *It's a Wonderful Life* (1946). And, of course, John Barrymore's granddaughter Drew continues to delight audiences to this day.

Norma Shearer

Short, cross-eyed and less than classically beautiful, she became one of Hollywood's most popular stars

Norma Shearer (below) was not the greatest beauty in Hollywood, but she may have been the most persistent. She endured endless eye exercises to overcome a decidedly cross-eyed stare. The director of the first feature in which she was slated to appear rejected her as "unphotogenic." Her next director reduced her to tears, but she turned in a performance that persuaded producer Irving Thalberg to cast her in six movies in eight months.

After MGM was founded in 1924, Shearer became one of the studio's most bankable stars, making 13 hit movies during the silent era. She made the transition to talkies seamlessly with box-office smashes like *The Divorcee* (1930), for which she won the Academy Award for best actress, and *A Free Soul* (1931), for which she was nominated. (She would be nominated as best actress six times.) After 1934, when the restrictive Motion Picture Production Code made it impossible for her to play sophisticated, sexually liberated women, Shearer starred in historical films, often playing "noble" characters like Marie Antoinette. When she retired in 1942, at age 40, her star power was undiminished.

Shearer and Thalberg married in 1927, and Shearer was deeply devoted to him until his untimely death in 1936. Shearer died in 1983, largely forgotten, more than 40 years after her last appearance onscreen.

THE ROARING '20s

EDITORIAL DIRECTOR Kostya Kennedy
EDITOR Eileen Daspin
DIRECTOR OF PHOTOGRAPHY Christina Lieberman
DESIGNER Ronnie Brandwein-Keats
PHOTO EDITOR Rachel Hatch
PHOTO ASSISTANT Steph Durante
COPY EDITOR Ben Ake (2020 edition)
RESEARCHER Emily Joshu (2020 edition)
PRODUCTION DESIGNER Sandra Jurevics
PREMEDIA TRAFFICKING SUPERVISOR Sarah Schuster
COLOR QUALITY ANALYST Heidi Parcel

MEREDITH SPECIAL INTEREST MEDIA
VICE PRESIDENT & GROUP PUBLISHER Scott Mortimer
VICE PRESIDENT, GROUP EDITORIAL DIRECTOR Stephen Orr
VICE PRESIDENT, MARKETING Jeremy Biloon
EXECUTIVE ACCOUNT DIRECTOR Doug Stark
DIRECTOR, BRAND MARKETING Jean Kennedy
ASSOCIATE DIRECTOR, BRAND MARKETING Bryan Christian
SENIOR BRAND MANAGER Katherine Barnet

EDITORIAL DIRECTOR Kostya Kennedy
CREATIVE DIRECTOR Gary Stewart
DIRECTOR OF PHOTOGRAPHY Christina Lieberman
EDITORIAL OPERATIONS DIRECTOR Jamie Roth Major
MANAGER, EDITORIAL OPERATIONS Gina Scauzillo

SPECIAL THANKS: Brad Beatson, Melissa Frankenberry, Samantha Lebofsky, Kate Roncinske, Laura Villano

MEREDITH NATIONAL MEDIA GROUP
PRESIDENT, MEREDITH MAGAZINES Doug Olson
PRESIDENT, CONSUMER PRODUCTS Tom Witschi
PRESIDENT, CHIEF DIGITAL OFFICER Catherine Levene
CHIEF REVENUE OFFICER Michael Brownstein
CHIEF MARKETING & DATA OFFICER Alysia Borsa
MARKETING & INTEGRATED COMMUNICATIONS Nancy Weber

SENIOR VICE PRESIDENTS
CONSUMER REVENUE Andy Wilson
CORPORATE SALES Brian Kightlinger
DIRECT MEDIA Patti Follo
RESEARCH SOLUTIONS Britta Cleveland
STRATEGIC SOURCING, NEWSSTAND, PRODUCTION Chuck Howell
DIGITAL SALES Marla Newman
THE FOUNDRY Matt Petersen
PRODUCT & TECHNOLOGY Justin Law

VICE PRESIDENTS
FINANCE Chris Susil
BUSINESS PLANNING & ANALYSIS Rob Silverstone
CONSUMER MARKETING Steve Crowe
BRAND LICENSING Steve Grune
CORPORATE COMMUNICATIONS Jill Davison
VICE PRESIDENT, GROUP EDITORIAL DIRECTOR Stephen Orr
DIRECTOR, EDITORIAL OPERATIONS & FINANCE Greg Kayko

MEREDITH CORPORATION
PRESIDENT & CHIEF EXECUTIVE OFFICER Tom Harty
CHIEF FINANCIAL OFFICER Joseph Ceryanec
CHIEF DEVELOPMENT OFFICER John Zieser
CHIEF STRATEGY OFFICER Daphne Kwon
PRESIDENT, MEREDITH LOCAL MEDIA GROUP Patrick McCreery
SENIOR VICE PRESIDENT, HUMAN RESOURCES Dina Nathanson
CHAIRMAN Stephen M. Lacy
VICE CHAIRMAN Mell Meredith Frazier

2017 EDITION
PRODUCED BY Kensington Media Group
EDITORIAL DIRECTOR Morin Bishop
DESIGNER Barbara Chilenskas
COPY EDITOR Joanne Camas

Published by Meredith Corporation • 225 Liberty Street • New York, NY 10281

Printed in the USA.

PHOTO CREDITS

COVER
(Clockwise from top left) John Kobal Foundation/Moviepix/Getty Images; Louis Van Oeyen/Western Reserve Historical Society/Getty Images; General Photographic Agency/Hulton Archive/Getty Images

BACK COVER
Courtesy of Missouri Historical Society, St. Louis

TITLE PAGE
P. 1: Keystone-France/Gamma-Keystone/Getty Images

CONTENTS
PP. 2–3: GraphicaArtis/Archive Photos/Getty Images

CHAPTER 1
PP. 4–5: The Granger Collection
P. 6: Universal History Archive/UIG/Getty Images
P. 7: George Rinhart/Corbis/Getty Images
P. 8: (From top) Dudley Shoe Co./The New York Historical Society/Getty Images; Library of Congress/Corbis/VCG/Getty Images; Stock Montage/Archive Photos/Getty Images; Independent Picture Service/UIG/Getty Images
P. 9: The Granger Collection
P. 10: Ullstein Bild/The Granger Collection
P. 11: Lipnitzki/Roger Viollet/Getty Images
P. 12: (From top) T.A. Edison, Inc./The New York Historical Society/Archive Photos/Getty Images; Edwin Levick/Hulton Archive/Archive Photos/Getty Images; Kirby/Topical Press Agency/Hulton Archive/Getty Images; National Motor Museum/Heritage Images/Hulton Archive/Getty Images
P. 13: Transcendental Graphics/Archive Photos/Getty Images
P. 14: General Photographic Agency/Hulton Archive/Getty Images
P. 15: Stock Montage/Archive Photos/Getty Images
P. 16: (From left) Mary Evans Picture Library/Everett Collection; Bettmann/Getty Images
P. 17: (Clockwise from top left) Pictorial Press Ltd./Alamy; Popperfoto/Getty Images; Advertising Archive/Courtesy Everett Collection (4)

CHAPTER 2
PP. 18–19: Bettmann/Getty Images
P. 20: Taglicht Media/Ullstein Bild/Getty Images
P. 21: Hulton Archive/Getty Images
P. 23: Bettmann/Getty Images
P. 24: Vintage Images/Archive Photos/Getty Images
P. 25: Underwood Archives/Archive Photos/Getty Images
P. 26: Armstrong Roberts/Classicstock/Everett Collection
P. 27: Ullstein Bild/Getty Images
P. 28 (From top) Universal History Archive/UIG/Getty Images; Jim Heimann Collection/Archive Photos/Getty Images
P. 29: Library of Congress
P. 30: Art Media/Print Collector/Getty Images
P. 31: Fox Photos/Hulton Archive/Getty Images

CHAPTER 3
PP. 32–33: Bettmann/Getty Images
P. 34: Universal History Archive/UIG/Getty Images
P. 35: Fotosearch/Archive Photos/Getty Images
P. 36: Kirn Vintage Stock/Corbis/Getty Images
P. 37: Chicago History Museum/Archive Photos/Getty Images
P. 39: Rue des Archives/The Granger Collection
P. 40: Underwood Archives/UIG/Everett Collection
P. 41: Edward Steichen/Conde Nast/Getty Images
P. 42: (From left) © Donna Mussenden VanDerZee; The Granger Collection
P. 43: (Clockwise from top left) Photo12/UIG/Getty Images; The Granger Collection; Mondadori Portfolio/Getty Images
P. 44, 45: Hulton Archive/Archive Photos/Getty Images
P. 46: Mary Evans Picture Library/Everett Collection
P. 47: Sasha/Hulton Archive/Getty Images

CHAPTER 4
PP. 48–49: Courtesy of Missouri Historical Society, St. Louis
P. 50: JP Jazz Archive/Redferns/Getty Images
P. 51: Hulton Archive/Getty Images
P. 52: AGIP/RDA/Everett Collection
P. 53: (From left) Hulton Archive/Archive Photos/Getty Images; John D. Kisch/Separate Cinema Archive/Moviepix/Getty Images; Edward Elcha/Michael Ochs Archives/Getty Images
P. 54: (From left) NY Daily News Archive/Getty Images; Bettmann/Getty Images
P. 55: Old Visuals/Alamy
P. 56: Edward Steichen/Conde Nast/Getty Images
P. 57: Bettmann/Getty Images
P. 58: PhotoQuest/Archive Photos/Getty Images
P. 59: Bettmann/Getty Images

CHAPTER 5
PP. 60–61: Bettmann/Getty Images
P. 62: Courtesy Everett Collection
P. 63: Keystone/FPG/Archive Photos/Getty Images
P. 64: The Ring Magazine/Getty Images
P. 65: (Top) Diamond Images/Getty Images
P. 67: George Rinhart/Corbis/Getty Images
P. 68: The Stanley Weston Archive/Archive Photos/Getty Images
P. 69: Mark Rucker/Transcendental Graphics/Getty Images
P. 70: Fox Photos/Hulton Archive/Getty Images
P. 71: Bettmann/Getty Images

CHAPTER 6
PP. 72–73: Bettmann/Getty Images
P. 74: Buyenlarge/Archive Photos/Getty Images
P. 75: Bettmann/Getty Images
P. 76: The Granger Collection
P. 77: Topical Press Agency/Getty Images
P. 78: Bettmann/Getty Images
P. 79: Chicago Tribune/TNS/Getty Images
P. 80: Jun Fujita/Topical Press Agency/Archive Photos/Getty Images
P. 81: Chicago Sun-Times/Chicago Daily News Collection/Chicago History Museum/Archive Photos/Getty Images (2)
PP. 82–83: Everett Collection
P. 84: John Kobal Foundation/Moviepix/Getty Images
P. 85: Ruth Harriet Louise/John Kobal Foundation/Moviepix/Getty Images
P. 86: Courtesy Everett Collection (2)
P. 87: Walter McBride/Corbis/Getty Images
P. 89: Bettmann/Getty Images
P. 90: Mondadori Portfolio/Getty Images
P. 91: (From top) Donaldson Collection/Moviepix/Getty Images; John Kobal Foundation/Mirrorpix/Getty Images
P. 92: (From top) General Photographic Agency/Hulton Archive/Getty Images; Eugene Robert Richee/John Kobal Foundation/Mirrorpix/Getty Images
P. 93: Courtesy Everett Collection (2)
P. 94: (From top) Sasha/Hulton Archive/Getty Images; Hulton Archive/Moviepix/Getty Images
P. 96: Kirn Vintage Stock/Corbis/Getty Images

SIGN OF THE TIMES
A couple stood with a traffic sign in Cordell, Oklahoma, circa 1920.

Printed in Great Britain
by Amazon

76259915R00056